Both thoughtful and courageous.

Dinesh D'Souza
Best-selling author, What's So Great About Christianity

Evangelicalism needs more books like *A Lover's Quarrel* to challenge its complacent acculturalization—because the gradual changes that have occurred during the last 40 years have not always been beneficial.

Luder Whitlock
President emeritus, Reformed Theological Seminary

For those who are truly serious about the implications of Christ's Great Commission, I highly recommend *A Lover's Quarrel.* This book is for all who are broken over the fact that our nation is spiritually bankrupt, despite a well-funded American Christian industry and thousands of Dolby-surround-sound-equipped churches. Reading it reminded me of what a doctor said to my father as he was about to undergo chemotherapy: "What you're about to experience will be painful, but it is necessary to save your life." I applaud Warren Smith's scholarship and courageous candor. I pray that many will give serious consideration to the content of his book.

Dr. Alex McFarland
President, Southern Evangelical Seminary
Author, The Ten Most Common Objections to Christianity

Warren Cole Smith's *A Lover's Quarrel with the Evangelical Church* recalls us to a once known but largely forgotten truth: that bad ideas have bad consequences despite good intentions. He is charitable with the evangelical church, but he reveals its deconstructions of orthodox understandings of Christianity. He speaks arrestingly of what it means to recover a valid sense of Christian community in its reality, not the technological spectacle of "virtual reality," however sincerely pursued.

Marion Montgomery
Author of more than two dozen works of criticism, fiction, and poetry

In his new book, Warren Cole Smith delves with grace and disturbing insight into the promise and bewildering failures of modern American evangelicalism. Writing from long experience within the movement, he reveals how evangelicals have succumbed to the glitter and material enticements of the world. Importantly, his "lover's quarrel" with evangelicalism also draws on other traditions—Christian and non-Christian—to show believers the way back to a surer grounding of the church in the Gospels.

Dr. Allan Carlson
President, The Howard Center for Family, Religion & Society

Words exchanged in lover's quarrels are best quickly forgotten, but the terms Warren Cole Smith uses to critique current evangelical excesses—"the Christian Industrial Complex," "Body-Count Evangelism"—should long be remembered. Smith points out that megachurches sometimes inflate their numbers, but even an accurate count may register only superficiality. Smith's call for churches to emphasize spiritual depth is worth hearing.

Dr. Marvin Olasky
Editor-in-chief, WORLD Magazine
Provost, The King's College

Warren Smith offers an insightful and deeply personal critique of the evangelical movement from the inside out. As a man of the movement, Smith's provocative assessment hits home. His penetrating analysis, however, goes beyond self-criticism and offers evangelicalism a pathway toward recovering its high-cultural heritage as a significant and vital movement of religious and social reform.

Alan R. Crippen, II
President, John Jay Institute

This is an important book for a crucial moment in our history as Christians in the United States. Besides being richly biblical in its analysis of contemporary evangelicalism, this book is written by a veteran journalist with hard-hitting and inescapable data to support his conclusions. I highly recommend this book.

Dr. Michael Horton
J. Gresham Machen Professor of Systematic Theology and Apologetics
Westminster Seminary California

Warren Cole Smith, a long-time member, spokesman, and activist in the American evangelical church, serves this same church well by calling attention to some of its besetting sins and flaws. What distinguishes Smith's critique from others is his use of Richard M. Weaver's *Ideas Have Consequences* (1948) to expose cultural and theological diseases in both evangelical churches and in the ubiquitous evangelical parachurch organizations. In *A Lover's Quarrel with the Evangelical Church*, Smith utilizes Weaver's perceptive, prophetic critique of modern American romanticism, sentimentality, and tradition-destroying reliance on mass media, to build up, not to tear down, the evangelical church.

Dr. Michael Jordan
Professor and chair, Department of English
Hillsdale College

Warren Cole Smith's *A Lover's Quarrel with the Evangelical Church* is the perfect dose of tough love that the evangelical community needs to become a better (and much more attractive) witness to the secular world. Warren easily wins the "quarrel" by using biblically based arguments backed by solid research that doesn't leave much wiggle-room for debate. It might make some Christians uncomfortable, which is exactly why they should read this book.

William Lobdell

Former religion editor, The Los Angeles Times
Author, Losing My Religion

For those who've scratched their heads and wondered how in the world evangelicalism arrived at its current state, this book opens some doors of insight. A compassionate tone overrides the temptation to cynicism, and in that context the author provides a narrative that I can't help but think will benefit defenders and naysayers of the movement alike.

Pat Terry

Contemporary Christian music pioneer

Warren Cole Smith, like a good tour guide, points out the sights and sounds of a troubled evangelicalism in ways that will make you want to get off the bus and look around. His keen and ironic sense of history makes points of interest take on a life of their own. For those concerned about evangelicalism, Smith's tour becomes one more reason to seek change. For those who didn't know evangelicalism was in trouble, his insights will be an important wake-up call. It's one of the most poignant and clearly written histories of evangelicalism and its connections that has been written in quite a while.

Dr. Michael A. Longinow
Professor and chair, Department of Journalism, Biola University

There are plenty of critics and blowhards who lob rhetorical bombs from a safe distance. But Warren Cole Smith has done something more rare and valuable. He has wrestled with both his conscience and with the mixed messages of his Christian tradition. The result is an honest, thoughtful, heartfelt, and provocative book that will challenge readers to do some similar wrestling of their own.

Steve Rabey
Writer and editor, Youthworker Journal

In his powerful, judicious, and constructive critique of evangelical churches, parachurch organizations, media, and culture, Warren Cole Smith demonstrates that many evangelicals have become addicted to size, speed, and power and have abandoned a biblical perspective of creation, history, and mission. Determined not simply to point out problems, but to help evangelicals regain a biblical focus and fulfill the evangelistic and cultural mandates more effectively, he provides positive examples of what some organizations and congregations are doing to further these aims.

Dr. Gary Scott Smith
Professor of history, Grove City College
Author, Faith and the Presidency: From George Washington to George W. Bush

A Lover's Quarrel is a riveting book that clearly separates real Christianity from both the feel-good movement and the money machines that drive much of modern evangelicalism. Who better to write this book than Mr. Smith, who has been a key opinion maker in the national evangelical movement? A careful yet truthful analysis of the church today. A must read for any thinking Christian.

Steve Maye
President, Lead With Character
Trustee, Erskine College

A LOVER'S QUARREL

WITH THE

EVANGELICAL CHURCH

WARREN COLE SMITH

A LOVER'S QUARREL

WITH THE

EVANGELICAL CHURCH

WARREN COLE SMITH

Authentic

COLORADO SPRINGS • MILTON KEYNES • HYDERABAD

Authentic Publishing
We welcome your questions and comments.

USA	1820 Jet Stream Drive, Colorado Springs, CO 80921
	www.authenticbooks.com
UK	9 Holdom Avenue, Bletchley, Milton Keynes, Bucks, MK1 1QR
	www.authenticmedia.co.uk
India	Logos Bhavan, Medchal Road, Jeedimetla Village, Secunderabad
	500 055, A.P.

A Lover's Quarrel with the Evangelical Church
ISBN-13: 978-1-60657-028-9

Copyright © 2008 by Warren Cole Smith

11 10 09 / 6 5 4 3 2 1

Published in 2009 by Authentic

A catalog record for this book is available through the Library of Congress.

Cover and interior design: projectluz.com
Editorial team: Bette Smyth, Daniel Johnson, Dana Bromley

Printed in the United States of America

CONTENTS

ACKNOWLEDGMENTS

Before I started writing, I had a sentimental picture of the writer as someone who, to paraphrase sportswriter Red Smith, opened a vein and spilled blood on the page. Maybe some people write that way. For me the process is very different. Sure, the physical creation of the thing does, indeed, involve solitary and sometimes soul-wrenching hours at the keyboard, but that's the least of it. The rest of it—the most of it—is quote gathering, fact checking, organizing, and reorganizing; getting advice from friends, knowledgeable readers, and editors; and then revising and revising again. Books, especially nonfiction books, are not so much written as built. And while I might be the general contractor, there was a whole crew that worked on this project.

So let me acknowledge a few people without whom this book would not have come to be.

I would first like to acknowledge the staff of World Newspaper Publishing, past and present, who helped me create the platform from which we could observe the world, and the evangelical church in particular. I would particularly like to acknowledge Jamie Dean, who served as a reporter and editor with me for many years before moving to WORLD Magazine. Her journalistic and theological compass continued to point true north even when my own would sometimes spin. The reporting she did on Joel Osteen, which was published in the *Charlotte World* as "Positively Dangerous," added a great deal to my discussion of Osteen in chapter three.

The idea for this book owes much to Brian Peterson of World Vision. I was one of four journalists who accompanied Brian to India in 2003 to see that ministry's work in the slums of Chennai (Madras) and Mumbai (Bombay). I said to Brian often on that trip, "If the evangelical church back home could see what we saw today, it would change everything." Brian encouraged and challenged me, "Make them see."

But see what? We see starving kids on our television screens every day. The real horror of the world today is that even those of us who say we care can walk right past our dying brothers and sisters with scarcely a second glance.

It was a second trip to India, in 2006, that crystallized for me what this book should be, gave me the bulk of chapter seven, and showed me what evangelicalism could become. That second trip was made with the remarkable Christian ministry Gospel for Asia. For that ministry's hospitality, I want to thank my guide on that trip, Taun Cortado, and Gospel for Asia's founder, Dr. K. P. Yohannan, who gave generously of his time and graciously answered my sometimes impertinent questions.

There are many others who encouraged me to write this book in particular, or just to write in general. I am grateful to you all but would like to mention a few who read various chapters when they were still quite rough and made helpful suggestions: Martin Davis, John Allen, my daughter Brittany Smith (who is becoming a fine writer herself), my sister-in-law Julie Smith, my sister Jackie Arthur, Dr. Michael Jordan of Hillsdale College, Jacie Crowell (who provided a paragraph-by-paragraph critique), and Steve Maye. Casey Moore, Laura Stidham, and Shari Anne Breuninger helped build the index. Marvin Olasky of WORLD Magazine provided valuable input and encouragement. Ed Pease read the manuscript in its late stages and caught problems that, if uncorrected, would have caused this writer much embarrassment. That said, errors undoubtedly remain. For these I take full responsibility.

To the team at Authentic Books I offer a special thanks. Volney James and Dana Carrington saw the potential of this book before many others could, and Bette Smyth, my editor, helped realize that potential. My gratitude runs deep and is still inadequate.

You will not read far in this book before you begin to recognize that I have borrowed heavily from the ideas of others. This book, in fact, should probably be seen as a kind of gloss on Richard Weaver's *Ideas Have Consequences*, Neil Postman's *Amusing Ourselves to Death*, and David Wells's *No Place for Truth*. If this book is helpful to you in any way, you should go read these books straightway. I offer this advice knowing full well that if you take me up on it you will know what an idea thief I really am. My only defense is Solomon's truism that there's nothing new under the sun. My greatest hope for this book is that I have taken their ideas and made them a bit more accessible.

It is impossible to say how much this book owes to Marion Montgomery, under whom I sat while a graduate student at the

University of Georgia a generation ago. I am a better writer and a better human being because of my time with him. His ideas, poured out in more than thirty books of his own, are on every page that follows.

And, of course, no list of acknowledgments would be complete without mentioning my wife, Missy, who sometimes encouraged me, sometimes cajoled me, and always did what she thought was necessary. I mentioned Brittany, who is beginning to get an inkling of what her father is up to. To my other children—Cole, Walker, and Morgan—I hope against hope that one day you think this book is worth all the time I spent away from you to write it.

TO BUILD UP,
NOT TO TEAR DOWN

I have spent a good deal of my life on airplanes. And in the days before September 11, 2001, when you could roam a bit more freely in airports, it was possible to get on and off airplanes at layover stops to meet family and friends at the gate, rather than at the baggage claim, and even to temporarily board planes to help others get settled. Then just before the doors of the plane would close, you would often hear an announcement that sounded something like this: "You are on Flight 123 to Atlanta. If you are not supposed to be on Flight 123 to Atlanta, please deplane at this time."

I once asked a flight attendant if that announcement was really necessary. Her reply was, "Oh yes. You'd be surprised."

It is with that experience in mind that I thought it only fair to let you know what our destination is with this book. In other words, who is supposed to be on this plane, where are we going, and how are we going to get there?

This book is intended primarily for Christian believers, particularly those who might generally fit into the category of theologically conservative, evangelical believers. Though much of what follows is highly critical—on both practical grounds and theological grounds—of the current state of the evangelical church, it is criticism aimed to build up, not to tear down.

But it must also be acknowledged that I approach this enterprise with the belief that much has gone wrong. And no wise builder would fail to clear the rubble before beginning afresh. He would demolish, haul away, and dig a new foundation. I have a friend who is both an experienced church planter and a seasoned construction executive, and he once shared with me an old saw of the construction business: "To build up, you first have to dig down, and the taller the building, the deeper the hole."

That is the task before us.

MY NAME IS WARREN, AND I'M A RECOVERING EVANGELICAL

I am a man who is very reluctantly and grudgingly, step by step, destroying myself so that this nation and the faith by which it lives may continue to exist. It is not a role I would have chosen for myself. I am merely doing the job as I see it. Someone, some way, had to come along and lift off the lid. Someone had to say, "This is what's inside." The man who lifts the lid has to testify just as much against himself as against anyone else.

—WHITTAKER CHAMBERS IN *WITNESS*

For most of my Christian life, I have considered myself an evangelical. From the time I made a public profession of faith in Christ at age fourteen and for most of my adult life until now, "evangelical" was a label I gladly wore.

The word *evangelical* was one I liked because it seemed to transcend secular politics and religious denominations. I could

1

claim kin with other evangelicals in denominations different from my own. I could disagree with someone about welfare reform or tax laws, but we could agree on the power of "Christ and him crucified" to save a lost and dying world, a world that includes you and me.

And being something of an amateur linguist, as most writers congenitally are, I appreciated its etymology. The word *evangelical* came into common usage only recently (in the twentieth century) and suggests the proclamation of the good news of Jesus. The word *angel*, which means "messenger," is at the very heart of the word, and at the very heart of my own vision for my life, as both a writer and a Christian. I wanted to be a messenger of good news.

So I thoroughly immersed myself in the evangelical movement. From street evangelism to small-group Bible studies to Promise Keepers, I did it all. In college at the University of Georgia in the 1970s, I had a Sunday morning program on the campus radio station where I played Larry Norman, Randy Stonehill, and Phil Keaggy. I may have been the first disc jockey in North America—certainly among the first—to play an Amy Grant song on the broadcast airwaves. I began to see Christian media, radio and television in particular, as a way to infiltrate and ultimately subjugate the secularist mindset that I believed had overtaken the country. And I wanted to be a part of that process.

But all the while I was also reading and seeing things that caused me disquiet. Harry Blamire's book *The Christian Mind* introduced me to the idea of a Christian worldview (though the book never used the phrase itself). I drove from Athens to

Atlanta one Friday afternoon in the late 1970s to hear evangelical icons Francis and Edith Schaeffer when they released their film series *How Should We Then Live?*, and I began to realize that the kind of culture they were wanting to see Christians be a part of and even champion was based on the highest and best traditions of Judeo-Christian civilization. But the evangelical movement was increasingly embracing low-brow, pop culture, so much so that Frank Schaeffer, Francis and Edith's son and their collaborator on that film series, renounced evangelicalism in favor of the Greek Orthodox faith.

I still believed in the great hope of evangelicalism, which is summarized in the Great Commission in Matthew 28:19–20: "Go and make disciples." But in the 1960s and '70s, many evangelical leaders succumbed to a sense of dread in the air. The cold war was at its height. Israel had become a nation in 1948, and many believed this was the last great prophetic fulfillment. Vietnam and Watergate created national anxiety. Books such as Hal Lindsey's apocalypse-predicting *The Late Great Planet Earth* were on the bestseller lists and were helping to define the theology of many evangelicals. When the Jesus Movement exploded on the scene, culminating—many say—with Explo '72, a giant evangelical gathering in Dallas, it felt to many as if the Holy Spirit was doing a great work.

But it didn't take many more years to realize how ephemeral the fruits of those years were. The Jesus Movement had been, in part, a response to the dead orthodoxy of the mainline church, a church that had lost the power to transform lives. But what the Jesus Movement evolved into was a lively heterodoxy that its often well-intentioned founders—many of whom were new converts and theologically illiterate themselves—could not control. Cults were founded or found a foothold. Heretical teachings infiltrated the mainstream church. Over time, as I suggested above, I began to grow skeptical over the conversion claims of some of the groups at the forefront of the movement. (It was becoming increasingly clear to me—based on mathematics alone—that filling out a decision card at a youth rally or stadium-style event is not necessarily a conversion.) Not only that, for every convert the evangelical movement created, it seemed to me, it left casualties—people who had grown skeptical or cynical about what they were seeing.

It was beginning to dawn on me that the Great Commission was a command to make disciples and teach them to obey the commands of Christ, not just tally up decisions like so many notches on a gun belt.

I also read Ron Sider's *Rich Christians in an Age of Hunger*. The solutions that Sider has gone on to advocate in his career as a spokesman for the religious left I find problematic, but his fundamental diagnosis derived directly from Scripture that true religion is to look after widows and orphans in their time of need (James 1:27) was deeply convicting to me—and something I did not see much of in the evangelical church. The evangelical church had spawned the megachurch. It had become about power building, not power sharing. And it certainly was not about power sacrificing. I began to wonder if the true religion that James said is pleasing to God was something other than the religion that I and my evangelical brothers and sisters were practicing.

I pursued a graduate degree in literature and then a career in writing and publishing, so I was forced to read widely outside of the Christian ghetto. Many of these books could not be found in a Christian bookstore but were deeply Christian in their worldview or at least had much to offer someone striving to develop a Christian worldview. For example, in 1977 Paul C. Vitz published *The Psychology of Religion: The Cult of Self-Worship*. Vitz described how *selfism*—or defining the world in terms of one's self rather than in terms of an objective or at least an external reference point—has infiltrated our culture and Christianity itself. Neil Postman's 1985 book, *Amusing Ourselves to Death*, helped me understand that one of the basic premises of modern evangelicalism—that you can use any method to communicate the gospel so long as you don't change the message—is ultimately a false and dangerous idea, because it is not possible. The medium really is the message. The words "Fear not. Jesus is Lord." spoken by a televangelist in order to get you to throw discernment and prudence to the wind and send him a "seed gift" is a very different message from the words "Fear not. Jesus is Lord." spoken softly by a pastor who holds your hand as you lie helplessly in the intensive care unit.

Both Vitz, who is a Christian, and Postman, who was not (he died in 2003), wrote much that was painful to read, about how this evangelical Christianity that I had embraced had gone astray. Painful to read, but it also had the ring of truth.

What was even more painful to me was the disintegration of the lives of too many of my evangelical friends. Many of my friends from college, young men and women from backgrounds like mine, who in their idealistic youth thought they could "take back this generation for Christ," were beginning to fall by the wayside. When Ted Haggard, the president of the National Association of Evangelicals (NAE), admitted in late 2006 he had fallen into drug abuse and a homosexual relationship,[1] he became emblematic of a disturbing number of people who I knew had been nurtured on the mother's milk of the evangelical subculture—who had, like me, plunged snout and forelegs into the trough of Christian music, rallies, and all the accoutrement found in a modern Christian bookstore—and were falling away from faith, not growing in faith.

Spiritually speaking, we fed on this pablum to the point of bloat, but we remained malnourished. Many of the friends I thought would grow up to be leaders in the church were falling into depression. Their marriages were breaking up. Some succumbed to homosexuality or other forms of sexual promiscuity, often with devastating effects on their emotional and family lives. Several men I knew in the Christian music industry saw their lives and careers disintegrate as a result of drug use.

To be sure, some—many—continued to serve Christ. My college roommate, Craig Kent, left the University of Georgia a year ahead of me for medical school. He is a surgeon who spent many years as a missionary in Africa, serving with the wife of his youth and four growing children. There are a host of others I could name who have gone on to serve God honorably—some of whom make appearances in the book that follows, providing an example of our way forward.

Even so, I could not dismiss a troubling pattern I was beginning to see in the lives of men and women who I thought would be stout warriors for the faith. Of course, I knew that Paul taught about a time when Christians must stop drinking milk and move on to the meat. And it occurred to me that this was what I was seeing. Was it merely that the church was offering milk and no meat? If that were so, it would be a cause for concern, but not so complicated a problem. Just start serving meat. That may be easier said than done, but at least you would know what you had to do. Again, if that was indeed the problem.

But I began to fear that the situation was worse than that. It was almost as if there was something toxic in the soil of the evangelical garden. It may be true that most churches serve milk, not meat. But it began to look to me as though even the milk was tainted. It looked rich and nourishing, and for a while, for many young Christians, it was. But it was almost as if, like milk that contains mercury or lead, the poison was building up over time.

And even the poison was hard to recognize. It was an unanswered doubt that slowly eroded faith. It was a quick condemnation of homosexuality or alcohol or gambling, but an indulgence of greed and envy in the form of careerism. It was the hypocrisy of religious-right political leaders quick (and right) to condemn big government and its corrupting power, but who thought that the big ministries and megachurches they were creating would somehow be immune to the same corrupting power. It was all this and a lot more. The data my life experience was gathering pointed to a troubling conclusion: the men and women I knew who were still growing in faith twenty years after they were first planted in this garden had, almost to a person, transplanted themselves outside of the evangelical milieu in some significant way.

Indeed, one of the more interesting of many religious movements taking place in this country today is the quiet movement of many evangelical leaders—Frank Schaeffer is by no means the only one—away from evangelical churches to more historical and liturgical expressions of faith. Billy Graham was a founder of *Christianity Today* magazine, but today many of its editors and contributors are Anglican or Orthodox. Some of those on the staff of Chuck Colson's organization are Anglican or Roman Catholic.

My question, quite simply, is, Why? What is it about evangelical theology or evangelical practice that is both so appealing and so troubling? I could not deny that I had seen much good come out of parachurch ministries and evangelical churches, so I was not willing to throw the baby out with the bathwater. But it was clear that I was less and less comfortable calling myself an evangelical if what I was seeing was what that word meant. I began, you might say, to develop a lover's quarrel with the evangelical church and evangelical theology and practice.

My quest to resolve that conflict took me, among other places, to the little mountain town of Weaverville, North Carolina.

Getting at the Root Causes

One of the largest parachurch ministries in the world, Young Life, has a large and beautiful facility called Windy Gap in the mountains of western North Carolina, near Weaverville, which is just north of Asheville.

Over the years, tens of thousands of teenagers have come by car, van, and bus to Windy Gap. They often must drive through or—now that the interstate is finished—around Weaverville on their way to Windy Gap. The kids themselves are mostly from affluent suburban schools surrounding Charlotte, Atlanta, Knoxville, Greenville, Nashville, and other New South, Bible Belt cities—cities whose growth and influence in media, finance, and manufacturing have quietly usurped Rust Belt cities in both demographic (and therefore political) as well as culture-shaping power.

So it's not surprising that these children of the New South who come to Windy Gap sometimes make fun of Weaverville, a town that still recalls the inferiority complex felt by the denizens of the Old South. Indeed, Weaverville is usually featured prominently in the skits performed by the Young Life staff members at nightly *club* meetings at Windy Gap. *Club* sounds more inclusive and less threatening than *Bible study* to the kids who come to Windy Gap. It is a time of song singing, joke telling, and skits that are crafted—as longtime Young Life staffers often said—to "earn the attention" of the kids, so the gospel can be presented to them. Most Windy Gap camp weekends culminate on Saturday night or Sunday morning with an opportunity for the kids to pray to receive Christ. Many thousands have done so.

But it was not at Windy Gap where I found the answers I was seeking. Indeed, the hundreds of thousands of kids and Young Life staff who have been to Windy Gap over the years would probably be surprised to learn that this town they often joke about was the birthplace of one of the great philosophers of the twentieth century, a man who had a powerful impact on the conservative movement that began in the 1950s and continues even today.

Richard Weaver, after whose family the town of Weaverville was named, published his landmark book, *Ideas Have Consequences*, in 1948, just a few years after the 1941 founding of Young Life by Jim Rayburn and about the time dozens of evangelical parachurch organizations began all across America.[2]

In some ways, of course, it is a bit ironic that Weaverville and Young Life should have histories that are so intertwined. Young Life is an organization that embraces kids with methods and techniques, music and video pulled directly from American culture. Richard Weaver's little book, by contrast, is a brilliant diagnosis of what has gone wrong with our culture. Though it was never a bestseller, neither has it ever been out of print even a single day since it was published over a half century ago; and during that half century, it has had an impact on successive generations of conservative and religious thinkers. It is a little book about big ideas, which it gives away with its now famous opening line: "This is another book about the dissolution of the West."[3]

Though Weaver was not a Christian believer, I recognized that his concern for the decline of Western civilization made us fellow travelers. Indeed, this dissolution of the West, which Weaver attempted to diagnose, was exactly the precipitating cause of American evangelicalism. Most evangelicals (including myself then) believe that the world is in decline, that from the perfection of the garden of Eden we have descended and will continue to do so until we arrive at a depth so low that only the return of Jesus can possibly make things right. Things are only getting worse.

That Jesus himself did not see it this way is an important point. Jesus prayed and told us to pray, "Your kingdom come, . . . on earth as it is in heaven." Jesus seemed to teach that things were getting—or at least could get—better. But Weaver was not concerned with unpacking evangelical theology. He was a historian, a philosopher, and a political scientist. He thought in terms of the rise and fall of civilizations, and his goal was to identify the cause of the decline that he was seeing in his own time.

Again, Weaver was no Christian, but he did acknowledge the existence of evil. And he had no trouble identifying specific evils. Weaver's critique of the state of the world blamed the tendency of people today to view the world as they would like it to be, not as it really is. Weaver called this romantic view of the world "sentimentality" and said it was the enemy of reality and truth. Weaver said that modern psychology had turned many of us into spoiled children who refused to humble ourselves to our betters but expected happiness and help to be either the result of a simple step-by-step formula or (better yet) just given to us as if a birthright. He reserved special condemnation for what he called "the Great Stereopticon," the modern media that for the first time in history combined words, pictures, and sound in a single experience that had the effect of "decomposing eternity," robbing its users of connections with each other, history, and posterity.

Reading Paul Vitz and Richard Weaver gave me a diagnosis of what had gone wrong with the world. The diagnosis is complex, but some of the manifestations are these: a sentimental and unrealistic view of the universe, how-to self-help books and programs that deal with symptoms but not causes, and a tranquilizing television.

Indeed, when I read Richard Weaver's sixty-year-old critique of the modern world and translated it into my own experience, a light bulb went on in my mind. Weaver was not describing a world from which evangelicalism offered deliverance. He was describing what modern evangelicalism had become!

In the Midst of a Dark Wood

If all or even some of what I have said so far is true, American evangelicalism, for all the good it has done, is in need of a modern reformation.

That is what this book is about. I call it a lover's quarrel with the evangelical church because I believe it is important to speak the truth as two lovers would. In a marriage, two become one. When a husband cuts his wife, he injures himself. So it is with the church. We are all members of the body of Christ. When one hurts, we all hurt. There is a unity and oneness to the body. Therefore, it is not the goal of this book to destroy, but to encourage, sharpen, and build.

So I write this book as one who is not on the outside looking in, but as one who has intentionally been on the inside for forty years. Though this book names the names of many evangelical leaders, it is important that you realize that I have not just reported, but have actively participated in, many of the activities I describe here.

But like the protagonist in Dante's *The Divine Comedy*, I came to myself in the midst of a dark wood. That dark wood is the American evangelical church. And like Dante's hero, we will go a-journeying out and up, not with Beatrice as a guide, but with many guides, Richard Weaver among them. And along the way, we will describe what we see.

All of this because there is no unity without truth. That is why the strategy of this book will be to pursue the truth about the evangelical church in as unblinking a manner as possible. To look into its very nature and name what we see.

We have a model for this pursuit of the truth, this quest for insight into the very nature of things, at the very beginning of Scripture. All we have to do is follow God's very first instructions to Adam in Genesis 2. After God had created Adam, he told him to work the land. God then brought all the animals to him and told him to name the animals. It was indeed a remarkable moment. Adam, in intimate communion with God, had each of God's creatures before him; and Adam—with perfect insight— looked into the very nature of each animal; and based on that insight, he named each animal. God validated Adam's work by saying, "Whatever the man called each living creature, that was its name."

Looking deeply into the very nature of things, and then rightly naming those things, is at the very heart of what it means to be human. It should be at the very center of any quest for the truth.

CHAPTER 1

THE EVANGELICAL MYTH

The problem with the modern American church is that it is far too "modern American" and not nearly enough "church."

—*STANLEY HAUERWAS*

This book is a partial telling of the story of how and why the American evangelical church became the richest, most powerful religious movement in history, while the country in which this movement took place—the United States—sank ever deeper into moral and spiritual confusion. It is also the story of the relationship between the two, of how, in fact, the rise of the modern evangelical church may actually have caused the confusion we now lament.

But this book, this journey into and through the evangelical church, might also give us ways out of that confusion. Perhaps, by God's grace, we will not abandon the greatest promises of the evangelical church, but see how they may come to pass. We might become like Dante's unnamed narrator in *The Divine Comedy*. He is unnamed because he is all of us, and he gives us one of the great opening lines in all of literature: "Midway this life, I came to myself in the midst of a dark wood."

So while it is true that the evangelical church is in the midst of a dark wood, it is also possible that we may come to ourselves and find our way through the inferno. But coming to ourselves means facing some hard facts and asking some tough questions. This chapter is about some of those hard facts and tough questions.

The Myth of Evangelical Growth

Let's begin by stating plainly what we might call *the evangelical myth*. It goes something like this:

> Since World War II, perhaps even because of the apocalyptic destruction of World War II, a revival has been under way. In the years before the war, the mainline church had succumbed to liberalism and heresy. But then a new thing happened. Parachurch organizations such as Campus Crusade for Christ, InterVarsity Christian Fellowship, and the Navigators began taking the gospel to college campuses that were burgeoning with G. I. Bill-financed student bodies. These college students graduated to become leaders of churches and business—and an ever-expanding roster of still newer Christian ministries. Overflowing Billy Graham

crusades, Explo '72 (the "Christian Woodstock"), the Jesus Music revolution of the 1970s—these were all signs of a revival not seen in the United States since the Second Great Awakening. Drug addicts and rock stars were getting saved. Beginning in the 1970s, churches were exploding in growth. And in 1980 these Christians also began to make themselves known at the ballot box. The hope of those early leaders—that this revival would be not just a religious movement but a cultural and societal movement—seemed to be coming to pass.

That's the myth. And like all myths, there is truth in it. But also like all myths, it is more of a hope than a history. And the more the hope diverges from the history, the more the myth becomes a fiction.

It is my argument that the evangelical myth is not yet a complete fiction, but it is nearly so. And here are just a few historical facts that suggest the vitality of the evangelical myth and that—sometimes paradoxically—point toward its destruction:

- In 2004 the *values voter* was credited with giving George W. Bush the margin of victory he needed for the presidency. This election was just the most dramatic of several in the past twenty-five years in which the religious voter was considered vital.

- According to the Hartford Institute for Religion Research, the number of Protestant megachurches in the United States (churches with more than 2,000 regular attenders) was less than a dozen in 1970, but more than 1,200 in 2004. Those numbers represent a literal hundredfold increase.[1]

- In 1998 there were nearly 750,000 religious and charitable tax-exempt organizations. The number had nearly doubled just in the previous decade alone. A majority of these organizations were evangelical parachurch organizations.[2]
- In 2004 Christian retail sales passed the $4.6-billion mark for the first time.[3]

So, measured in terms of power and money, the evangelical church has never been healthier. But has the evangelical church, or the broader Christian church, really grown? Not if you consider some other, equally credible, measurements.

- According to a 2000 survey by Glenmary Research Center, between 25 and 30 percent of Americans called themselves evangelical. However, in 1980, according to James Davison Hunter, 31.7 percent of Americans were evangelical. And, interestingly, Hunter said that in 1900, 41 percent of Americans were evangelical. In short, it appears that the percentage of Americans who are evangelical actually declined significantly during the past century.[4]
- In 1900 there were twenty-seven churches per 10,000 Americans. In 1985 there were only twelve churches per 10,000. *Baptist Church Planting* magazine estimated the number of churches per 10,000 Americans today at less than ten.[5]

- In the decade of the 1990s, 4,000 American churches shut their doors permanently each year. In a typical year, less than half that many new churches were started.[6]
- The Barna Research Group found that while a substantial majority of Americans claimed to be Christian, and more than a quarter claimed to be evangelical, only about 9 percent believed such core doctrines of the Christian faith as the deity of Christ, the resurrection, and the authority of Scripture.[7]

While these data points neither prove nor disprove anything definitively, they should suggest to any honest inquirer that the much-touted growth of evangelicalism is not all that it appears to be.

Many evangelicals find it difficult to face these facts in part because their own economic and emotional self-interests are linked to the myth. According to *CPA Journal*, 7 percent of the U.S. work force works for either a church or a religious nonprofit organization.[8] Because the employees of nonprofits often share the organization's values and beliefs, it is likely that the percentage of evangelicals who make their living directly from the evangelical movement is much greater than 7 percent. And evangelicals who do not make a living from what I describe in chapter four as the Christian-industrial complex are financial contributors to it. So facing the possibility that the evangelical movement is having no impact or a negative impact on the spiritual life of the church or of the United States is a difficult possibility to admit.

But that is exactly the possibility we must face if we are to be honest with ourselves and if we are to recover our witness in a world that increasingly looks at evangelical Christians with disdain. So let's turn our attention not to a complete history of how money and power have turned the evangelical myth into a fiction, but to a few key chapters that are emblematic of the whole.

The Myth of Evangelical Political Power

Labor Day, in election years, is supposed to be the beginning of the campaign season. But in the nonstop campaign cycle that federal elections have become, Labor Day is more accurately the beginning of the final stretch of the political season. After Labor Day is when most of the money gets spent and most of the public activity takes place. It's when most of the campaigns go into high gear.

But it's possible that by Labor Day 2004 the presidential race was already over, though no one knew it then. It is also possible, given the repudiation of Republicans in the 2006 and 2008 elections, that this weekend may end up becoming the high-water mark for the impact of American evangelicalism on the political process—or at least on the Republican Party.

Just a few days earlier, Christian music star Michael W. Smith had played a prominent role as a performer at the Republican National Convention in New York City. Indeed, one of his songs was played just as George W. Bush came out to deliver his acceptance speech, which was the climax of the convention. In the minds of many evangelicals, it was a symbolic moment. The pop band Fleetwood Mac—known for a long string of Top 40 hits and for drug use, songs that suggested the occult, and the bed-hopping of its members—had provided the musical soundtrack for the Bill Clinton presidency. To have Michael W. Smith on the podium symbolized for many how far evangelical Christianity had come.

But by Labor Day weekend, Bush's convention bounce was beginning to fade. And, in fact, his ties to the religious right were energizing the Kerry campaign. Liberal Democrats, for good reasons or not, feared the evangelical movement.

The only real question was, Who would turn out to vote when election day came?

Dr. James Dobson, the president of Focus on the Family, wanted to make sure that Christians turned out, and he wanted to make sure that, if that did happen, Christian voters got the credit they deserved. So he decided that Labor Day, the official beginning of a campaign season that had already been two years long, would be the right weekend to flex his political muscle, the muscle of his organization, and the muscle of the evangelical church. Through an organization he had just created, Focus on the Family Action, he organized two Stand for the Family rallies in North Carolina. They would be the first of six such rallies he would hold between Labor Day and election day.

On the other side of the political battle line, the John Kerry campaign was in disarray. On the Saturday before Labor Day, things were so disorganized inside the Kerry campaign that senior aides to the Democrat's campaign forced the candidate to speak with ex-President Clinton, who was in a hospital room in New York, awaiting heart surgery. Clinton proceeded to lecture Kerry, with campaign aides listening in, on what he needed to do to get back in the presidential race. On Labor Day Monday, an account of that phone call made the front page of the *New York Times*.

That very evening, more than six thousand people gathered in Cricket Arena in Charlotte, North Carolina, for the first Stand for the Family rally.[9] The next night, with no competition from the Labor Day holiday, more than twelve thousand gathered in Raleigh. Dr. James Dobson, Bishop Wellington Boone, former presidential candidate Gary Bauer, and Family Research Council president Tony Perkins told both crowds to "vote their values." In part because of these rallies, Republican Richard Burr came from behind to defeat former Clinton Chief of Staff Erskine Bowles for the seat in the U.S. Senate previously held by John Edwards. The success of these North Carolina rallies encouraged Dobson to hold similar rallies in South Dakota, where John Thune would defeat incumbent Democrat Senator Tom Daschle in the most-watched Senate race in the nation.

These rallies were barely mentioned in the mainstream media on the days they occurred, but after the election they were cited in a *U.S. News and World Report* profile on James Dobson as both an indication of Dobson's ability to draw a crowd of evangelicals and an early sign that this year's election would be defined by what came to be known as the *values voter*. And within two years they were recognized as being defining moments in at least two books highly critical of the evangelical movement's close ties with the political process.[10]

These Stand for the Family rallies were believed to be so successful in the 2004 election cycle, that Focus on the Family, the Family Research Council, and allied groups began to plan them for the 2006 cycle. But things were changing in the political world. Republicans, with whom Dobson, Perkins, and others had aligned their political fortunes, were having big problems. After twelve years in power, Republican congressional leaders were once again proving the adage of Lord Acton that power tends to corrupt and absolute power corrupts absolutely.

This corruption and the subsequent fall from power were embodied by Jack Abramoff. Though Jack Abramoff is even now a relatively young man (he was born in 1959), he was active in conservative politics for more than two decades and, though Abramoff himself claims to be an Orthodox Jew, was closely aligned with the religious right for much of that time.

In fact, *Atlanta Weekly* magazine did a 1985 profile of a number of young conservatives called "Right Turn on Campus" that was in some ways prophetic.[11] I was living in Atlanta when the article was published. Because I had been an undergraduate acquaintance of Ralph Reed, one of the figures profiled in the article, I saved the magazine, which was actually an insert in the Atlanta paper. The yellowing newsprint, complete with a photo of local-boy Reed on the cover, told a story that—given what has happened in the intervening twenty years—is surreal to read today. It featured Abramoff most prominently. Abramoff by then had become a national figure as the chairman of the

College Republican National Committee. And he had risen to power in part because of the help of Ralph Reed, who later became president of the Christian Coalition and led it to national prominence.

Reed, however, was not a Christian when he moved to Washington in 1981 to serve as an intern for Abramoff. Indeed, Dan Gilgoff's book *The Jesus Machine* described the Ralph Reed I knew in those days as a "hard-drinking blowhard."[12] He was a conservative, one of the leaders of the Young Republicans at the University of Georgia, when I first met him, and we were both involved in campus politics. I remember that we talked about religion and abortion, which was the issue that got many religious conservatives involved in the Republican Party. But even then it was clear that Reed had bigger aspirations than simply manning a table in front of Memorial Hall (the student union at UGA in those days) to pass out fliers for the Young Republicans. Reed also made it clear to me then that religious guys like me had better wake up. That abortion was just the tip of the iceberg. That if the leftists were able and willing to commit abortion, there was no atrocity they would be unwilling to commit. Conservatives had to get organized and get ready to fight. A few years later, a cheesy, B-movie called *Red Dawn* was making the rounds at movie theaters. In it the Soviet Union had overrun the United States, and a group of young people led by Patrick Swayze had formed themselves into a band of guerrilla warriors who would continue the fight, by any means possible, from hideouts in the Rocky Mountains. That movie, indeed, had been produced by Abramoff. In fact, the movie became a symbol of the movement.

Reed's most memorable quote in the *Atlanta Weekly* article was, "We are the Red Dawn generation."

Such was the mindset of Reed and Abramoff in those days, a mindset they brought to their Washington activism. For young people, in particular, Washington can be the combination of a hot-box and a time machine. Washington years, some quip, are like dog years—one year equals seven. That's in part because young people live two days for every one spent there. The first day is at the office, and the second day begins at 5:00 PM with parties and receptions that can sometimes go into the next morning. Even interns, when they leave their cubicles at the end of the day and walk out onto the street and see the dome of the Capitol or the Washington Monument, cannot help but believe they are a part of something important.

Especially in those early years of the Reagan administration, young conservatives believed they were part of a revolution that would be history making. But the Red Dawn generation would not have to fight in conditions of privation from behind bunkers in some mountain fastness. They could fire their volleys from K Street. They would network at Washington cocktail parties. They would debate ideas with members of Congress and policymakers. In this atmosphere Reed and Abramoff became close friends. Reed even introduced Abramoff to the young woman who would eventually become Abramoff's wife.

But the atmosphere can also be physically and emotionally exhausting. Another legend about Washington is that you last either eighteen months or eighteen years. Reed was one of those who lasted closer to eighteen months. He had a conversion to

Christianity while interning for Abramoff in Washington, DC.[13] That conversion experience changed the course of Reed's life in many ways. His political ardor did not cool, but for a few years it rechanneled itself. He left Washington and returned to Georgia, receiving a Ph.D. in history from Atlanta's Emory University. Ironically, though Reed had counseled Christians to expand their political interests beyond abortion, he himself became a pro-life activist, even getting arrested outside an abortion facility in Raleigh, North Carolina.

The combination of his early Washington connections, his newly minted doctorate, and his pro-life bona fides brought him to the attention of Pat Robertson, who founded the Christian Coalition in the wake of Jerry Falwell's Moral Majority, which was winding itself down. Reed became the driving force behind the Christian Coalition. During its peak years, the Christian Coalition had an annual budget of $25 million and was responsible for supporting strong state chapters that in some cases—especially in the South—changed the shape of local and statewide politics.

Reed and Abramoff were often identified with their friend Grover Norquist. Together, they were the very personification of the three-legged stool that conservative gurus said made up the Reagan Coalition: defense conservatives, religious conservatives, and fiscal conservatives. Abramoff brought the money connections and the Red Dawn national security patriots; Reed's association with the Christian Coalition brought the voters of the religious right; and Norquist became executive director of Americans for Tax Reform, an organization known for a plan to dramatically reduce the size of the federal government. He became famous for saying he was not opposed to government, but "I want it small enough so I can drag it to the bathroom and drown it in the tub." Norquist's star would shine even brighter when it became known that he was a key strategist and coauthor of Newt Gingrich's 1994 Contract with America.

The relationship between Abramoff, Reed, and Norquist was perfect for all three. Reed and Norquist could remain ideologically pure, above the fund-raising fray. So throughout the 1980s, '90s, and into the new century, Reed and Norquist could go to Abramoff for money, and Abramoff could go to Reed for votes and to Norquist for strategy and ideas.

Ralph Reed always had the highest profile of the three, eventually landing on the cover of *TIME* magazine in May 1995 under the headline "The Right Hand of God."[14] So it was no surprise to anyone when he decided that he wanted to run for office himself. Not long after making the *TIME* cover, in December 1997, Reed resigned from the Christian Coalition, moved back to Georgia, and began to lay the groundwork for his own political career. He formed Century Strategies, which became known for a series of highly controversial and mostly unsuccessful political campaigns in the 1998 and 2000 election cycles. But one success covered a multitude of sins, and that success was becoming a key strategist in George W. Bush's 2000 presidential campaign.

When John McCain won the 2000 New Hampshire primary, he immediately moved to front-runner status. The next major proving ground would be in South Carolina. McCain had momentum, and if he could win in South Carolina, conventional wisdom was that he would sweep to the Republican nomination. Many religious conservatives had not committed to either Bush or McCain because of the presence of both Gary Bauer and Alan Keyes in the race. The picture was further complicated when Bauer dropped out of the race and surprised many by endorsing McCain. Reed masterminded a Bush victory in South Carolina, which put the brakes on the McCain campaign and caused Bush to emerge as the candidate of choice for the religious right.[15]

It was a defining moment for both the Bush campaign and Ralph Reed. When Bush ultimately moved into the White House, Reed became known as something of a kingmaker. He was elected chairman of the Georgia Republican Party in 2001; and in the 2002 and 2004 elections, under Reed's leadership, Republicans showed significant gains in the state, electing a Republican governor and replacing Democrat senators with Republican senators in Washington.

When Reed began looking for an office for himself, one that could eventually propel him, possibly, even to the presidency, some were surprised that he chose to pursue Georgia's lieutenant governor's chair. But, in fact, his strategic acumen was on full display in that choice. For the past forty years, presidents have mostly been former governors, not former senators or representatives. Georgia was a perfect state from which to launch a national bid. Carter had done it, and in the intervening thirty years, Atlanta had become a powerhouse business and money center. And in Georgia the lieutenant governor's chair was the right platform from which to run for governor. In some states the "lite guv" is largely a ceremonial position, but in Georgia it is anything but that. The lieutenant governor presides over the state senate and is therefore one of the most powerful elected officials in the state. Zell Miller, for example, used his tenure as lieutenant governor to further a political career that ultimately yielded two terms as governor and one in the U.S. Senate.

Reed began campaigning almost immediately after the 2004 election and was an early front-runner. I spoke with Reed in late 2005, and he told me that he would have to raise more than $4 million. A lot of money, but less than half of what he would have to raise to run for governor. He was well on his way to doing that on New Year's Day 2006.

But that's when things started going badly for Reed, Abramoff, and the values-voter brand that had been so carefully crafted and used to good effect in 2004.

On January 3—the first real business day of this midterm election year—Abramoff pled guilty to three felony counts in a Washington, DC, federal court. The next day he pled guilty to two more felony counts in a Florida court. It had already been revealed that Reed's Century Strategies had taken fees from Abramoff. At first glance, the fees were not unlike other dealings between Abramoff and Reed. Reed, maintaining his ideological purity, had been involved in several efforts to curtail gambling. So when Abramoff paid him to help curtail casino gambling . . . well, so far, so good. But then it was revealed by WORLD Magazine and others that Abramoff had been paid by a Native

American casino to squash competition from other casinos. So, in reality, the goal was not to stand against gambling, but to stand against competition for those already getting rich off gambling.

The ties to Abramoff tarnished Reed's fund-raising efforts. When I interviewed Reed in late 2005, he could still maintain the illusion that he was the front-runner. But what he must have known even then was that his fund-raising was beginning to dry up. A few days after Abramoff was indicted, Reed's fourth-quarter 2005 financial disclosure statements were made public, and they showed that he was getting badly beaten in fund-raising by the only Republican still in the race, state Senator Casey Cagle.

And to add insult to injury, President Bush visited Georgia in July 2006 just days before the primary election and all but ignored Reed, saying that as long as there was another Republican in the race, he would not take sides. Reed tried to salvage his campaign by inviting Rudolph Guiliani to campaign for him. To many of Reed's former supporters, it was a sign of desperation—and a sign that Reed had completely sold out his Christian values. Guiliani was both pro-choice and pro-gay. He was the kind of Republican that Reed and his supporters in previous years would have worked against.

When the primary was held, Reed was badly beaten by Cagle, 56 percent to 44 percent. A disappointed Reed told reporters he would likely never seek public office again.

Reed's defeat was a precursor of the November 2006 election, when Republicans lost both houses of Congress and many other seats in local and regional elections. Theories abounded and arguments continue about why the Republicans were beaten so badly. Surely, the Abramoff affair contributed. Just weeks before the election, it was revealed that U.S. Representative Mark Foley had sent sexually suggestive e-mails to House pages. It was suggested that Republican leaders knew of Foley's indiscretions and did not do enough to discipline him. The party of the Moral Majority, the Christian Coalition, and the religious right had become the party of fraud and moral failure. The war in Iraq was not going well at election time. These factors and more served to discourage Republicans and encourage Democrats to turn out.

But conservatives, and Christian conservatives in particular, needed neither Foley nor Abramoff to indicate that the Republican Party was no longer their true home. Pro-lifers have grown increasingly discouraged by the Republican Party's inability to make any meaningful headway on the abortion issue. Those who considered themselves classical conservatives were horrified by the "big-government conservatism" of the Bush administration, which enlarged both the size of the government and the size of the national debt. In times of crisis people want grownups in charge. It was getting harder and harder to figure out who the grownups were.

But the leaders of the evangelical movement were among the last ones to get the message. Jack Abramoff got a powerful message that the party was over when he was convicted of federal crimes. Ralph Reed got the message when he was badly defeated. But Focus on the Family and the Family Research Council continued apace. They held their annual Washington

Briefing just weeks before the election. Almost two thousand people gathered at the Omni Shoreham Hotel. If the event had a star, it was George Allen. He came to speak at the event, and he stayed to mingle and to give interviews with everyone from the *New York Times* to a wide variety of Christian media outlets. Though Allen was in a race to keep his U.S. Senate seat, he was simultaneously trying to establish himself as the candidate of the values voter for the 2008 presidential campaign, and at least at this event, he was accomplishing that very goal. Everywhere Allen went cameras and lights and a press gaggle followed him—including me. I turned aside from the Allen entourage to interview Tony Perkins, the president of the Family Research Council and the official convener of the event. I asked Perkins how he thought Republicans would do in the election. Now, to be fair to Perkins, I asked him this question before the Foley scandal broke, but his answer shocked me. "The Republicans will hold their own," Perkins said. "We might even pick up a seat."

Needless to say, that didn't happen. The 2006 election was one of the worst elections in political history for the Republican Party.

It's possible that Perkins knew that things were trending badly for the Republican Party, and he was attempting to rally the troops. Said another way, it is possible that Perkins was intentionally lying. But it is much more likely that Perkins was simply fooled by the hype he had helped create at such events as the Stand for the Family rallies and the Washington Briefing. That's a more charitable and probably more accurate interpretation.

However, in the world of the Washington power game, where Tony Perkins and many other evangelicals have chosen to play, it is not at all clear which is better—being thought a liar or being thought a fool.

Of course, neither Tony Perkins, Ralph Reed, nor any other evangelical who throws himself or herself into this spin machine enters as either a liar or a fool, but that may be what the process produces. It is alleged that Adlai Stevenson, who ran unsuccessfully for president, ruefully summed up the experience: "Any man who will do what is necessary to become president is automatically unfit to serve." If that is true of the presidency, it is also likely true to a lesser degree for any position of power in our current system.[16]

But why should this be so? Is it not possible to serve honorably? That we must ask the question or that its answer is not self-evident is an indicator of the current state of things. Did not Jesus say his kingdom is not of this world?

But even leaving Scripture aside, we know the answer to that question; we just don't think it applies to us. Many Christians have rightly criticized a liberal-leaning media and politicians for their ideological spinning of facts and the truth. Likewise, Christians have been rightly apprehensive of the concentration of power in an ever-expanding government, in part because of the morally and spiritually corrosive effects of concentrated power. Yet here was Tony Perkins doing exactly what he spends most of his time criticizing leftist ideologues for doing. He has become what he hates, or at least what he fights. And as we shall see, he is not alone.

So the quest for power tends to corrupt those who embark on the quest, and it is easy to see in the story we have just recounted how that quest for power could have so easily derailed the evangelical myth—despite the best intentions of those who began the journey.

The Myth of the Evangelical Market

The quest for money also tends to corrupt. Again, this should be no surprise to those who study Scripture, which teaches us that the love of money is the root of all evil. But it often appears that it is *other people's* love for money, and not our own, that is the problem.

The Stand for the Family rallies provide an inkling of what's involved. For these rallies, Focus on the Family set up mobile bookstores that did a brisk business

But the truth is that the Stand for the Family rallies were pretty noncommercial compared with other of the Christian traveling road shows. Take Promise Keepers, for example. When Promise Keepers began in the early 1990s, it was a local men's group, founded by the football coach at the University of Colorado, Bill McCartney, better known as Coach Mac. But from the very beginning the group had aspirations of scale, and with its combination of sports celebrities and big-name evangelical speakers, it didn't take long for the group to catch a wave. By the mid-'90s, it was packing arenas that held fifty thousand people or more. And on October 4, 1997, Promise Keepers organized the Stand in the Gap rally in Washington, DC. A million men attended that event.

Women have their own, slightly more evolved, version of these rallies called Women of Faith. Women of Faith, however, is a for-profit organization now owned by Thomas Nelson. It spawned The Revolve Tour, a rally for "tween" and teenage girls that is marketed directly to the girls and to their moms at the Women of Faith events.

Also targeting teenagers is Teen Mania's Acquire the Fire conferences, which draw thousands per city and typically do between twenty and thirty city tours each year.

Though all of these groups are different, there are several common threads running through them. One is that they all have significant merchandising arms. What goes on in the arena is just a part of the activity at these events. Everything from books and CDs to clothing and seats on Christian cruises are typically sold at the booths lining the concourses at these events. The result of all of this is big money: at its peak, Promise Keepers had an annual revenue of more than $100 million. In total, more than $1 billion has been funneled to the group since it was founded in 1990. Women of Faith takes in more than $50 million a year. Teen Mania has revenue of nearly $25 million a year. (All of these figures come from the public filings of the organizations themselves.)

Another characteristic of these organizations is that they have made their founders and key leaders what some would consider wealthy. Some of the more flamboyant televangelists, such as Benny Hinn, Joyce Meyer, and Trinity Broadcasting Network's Paul Crouch, have been famously investigated by watchdog groups and media organizations such as MinistryWatch.com, the

Los Angeles Times, and others. These investigations have revealed that these three ministry leaders, in particular, have benefited personally in the tens of millions of dollars.[17]

The gold standard for mass rallies has been Billy Graham. Indeed, Graham has, over a more than sixty-year career, kept himself and his organization remarkably free from scandal. Graham's own salary, while a comfortable six-figure income, is modest relative to others who lead organizations anywhere near the size of the Billy Graham Evangelistic Association, which in 2005 took in about $137 million in revenues.[18]

But Graham's son Franklin, who is now the president of Billy Graham Evangelistic Association as well as Samaritan's Purse, receives a total compensation from the two organizations that exceeds one-half million dollars, according to the two ministries' public filings. In the 1990s Samaritan's Purse had its membership in the Evangelical Council for Financial Accountability (ECFA) suspended. The ECFA said Samaritan's Purse didn't meet its standards related to board accountability and governance, Franklin Graham's use of ministry planes for personal use, and other issues. We should also note, though, that these matters were addressed by the ministry and that Samaritan's Purse is now a member in good standing in the ECFA.[19]

Another characteristic of these organizations and the mass rallies they produce is the degree to which these rallies have tapped directly into the local churches. The most successful of these events are often sold out weeks and months in advance because of bulk sales to churches. In other words, churches assume a good deal of the financial risk for these events by buying blocks of tickets at a discounted rate in order to resell them to church members from tables set up in foyers and fellowship halls in the weeks and months prior to the event. If the church is not able to resell the tickets to its members, it either gives them away or the seats remain empty. It is not unusual for an event that is officially sold out to have 20 percent of the seats go unused.

But perhaps the most important characteristic of these rallies is their ability to create the expectation of instant gratification—an expectation that your life will change, that your church will change, that your city will change . . . if you're a part of these events. And it's hard not to get caught up in the moment of these highly produced events. With heart-tugging video presentations, evangelicalism's most polished speakers, teeth-rattling music, sophisticated lighting, and a carefully crafted flow, an emotional response is virtually ensured. People usually don't walk out of a Promise Keepers or Women of Faith event saying they didn't get their money's worth.

But was the emotional rush a true spiritual change? We'll defer a definitive answer to that question, except to repeat what we said at the beginning of this chapter, that the long-lasting effects on the broader culture of these rallies are almost impossible to find. And, indeed, as the popularity of such events grows, the overall spirituality of the United States seems to be in decline.

But what is important to see, if we are to get to the definitive answer, are the several traits of modern evangelicalism at work. First and most obvious is simply the idea of mass or scale. In the next chapter we will look specifically at the phenomenon of the megachurch, which is this idea of scale applied in a particular motif—the local church—and taken to its logical end. It is enough to say here that in the calculus of the evangelical mind, large numbers are better, because it means that God is blessing the effort.

2nd Even better than large numbers is rapid growth, because even though you're not big yet, if you're growing, you'll get big soon enough. And bigness, even evangelicals will concede (usually when talking about mainline denominations or the Catholic Church), can lead to stagnation and death. But growth is a sign of life, and God is life; so growth is yet another sign of God's blessing.

A third essential ingredient of the mass rally is the role of money and corporations. The organization of these rallies is not cheap, and they can be very profitable. We have already seen how for-profit corporations have become instrumental in the organization of some of these events. But even those that remain under the umbrella of not-for-profit organizations have taken on the characteristics of the corporation. Focus on the Family's 2005 revenue was about $138 million. The Billy Graham Evangelistic Association has more variability in its annual budget than many organizations, depending on the number of rallies it conducts in a given year. But its 2006 revenue exceeded $130 million, and it had a whopping $296 million in assets. (All these figures come from the ministries' own public filings.)

Fourth, is their ability to stand apart from the local church—or, for that matter, from virtually everyone else—when it comes to oversight and accountability. In 1970 there were

Seems similar to
Big Ag & Small Farms

only about a dozen megachurches, and all of them were part of a denomination and governed by that denomination's polity (church law). Today, according to *Outreach* magazine's annual list of megachurches, approximately 25 percent of the thirteen hundred megachurches are nondenominational. Many of these do not have independent boards of directors. Some of them do not have deacons or elders. Most parachurch ministries are 501(c)(3) organizations, meaning they enjoy a tax-exempt status. However, many of them also claim to be churches and are thereby exempt from financial disclosure. And, of course, these facts relate just to financial accountability, saying nothing about spiritual or doctrinal accountability.

The final characteristic of the mass rally and the organizations behind them is the one that is the most difficult to talk about, but which is in many ways the most significant: their insistence on creating a community-altering moment. Most evangelical mass rallies, whether explicitly evangelistic or not, are billed as potentially historic events. The Billy Graham Evangelistic Association (BGEA) uses the word *historic* or *historical* to describe almost all of its crusades and many of its other activities. Typical is this headline from a BGEA press release describing a 2005 crusade in New York: "Billy Graham's Historic New York City Crusade to Be Broadcast in December." The press release goes on to describe the television broadcast schedule of a June 2005 crusade. It is one of dozens of uses of the word *historic* by the Graham organization to describe the organization's activities.

One of the ironies here is that this impulse to create the historic moment springs in part from our lack of, and a desire for, historicity, a phenomenon I call the *new provincialism*, which I explicate in greater detail in chapter two. What I will say here is that, like much we will discuss in this book and much that is a part of the evangelical myth, mass rallies were developed to respond to a real need—the widely felt need in the aftermath of a world blown apart by war and technology to create connectedness, community, and significance. But—again, like much we will discuss in this book and much that is a part of the evangelical myth—technologies and systems became the mechanistic substitutes for relationships and community. Size, speed, and power have become the ways the evangelical church measures God's blessing.

Becoming What We Hate

We began this chapter with a few data points about modern evangelicalism. We followed these data points with a few stories emblematic of the power and influence of evangelicalism. In pursuing this strategy, I am aware that if I draw conclusions based just on what we have seen so far, I am in danger of committing the same errors I am criticizing. I do not want to offer "anecdote as proof," or a single data point as a complete data set.[20]

But I do believe we have gotten to the point where it is fair to say this: many of the worse elements of the modern world—materialism, empire building at the expense of community building, and the accumulation of power and money—have become some of the most recognizable attributes of American evangelicalism. I have called American evangelicalism's growth and its accumulation of power and money "myths" not because there is not an element of truth in them, but because they don't tell the whole story. They tell merely the story we—some of us—want to believe about ourselves. But, as our brief discussion of this myth makes clear, there is also a dark side to the American evangelical myth.

That is not to say that there is not also much to admire about the modern evangelical movement: its desire and willingness to change the culture for good, for example. The power it has accumulated has been used at times effectively to stand against some of the darker angels of our nature. But too often we have spent the moral capital our history and theology have accumulated in our behalf just to buy a seat at the table of power. And once there, as Ralph Reed among many others has demonstrated, we have no power left to resist the temptations of that table.

Let me close this chapter with this idea: Evangelical Christians, at their best, are not unlike artists. They—we—are generative and procreative. Our goal is to lead those lost in an ugly and false view of the world toward beauty and truth.

But in order to fully realize this vision, we must confront what has sometimes been called "the devil in the inkpot." In other words, the artist who would tell the truth about the world must not shrink from the reality of evil. We evangelicals are good at pointing out the evil of others, but sometimes we forget that the best place to find evidence of original sin is to look in the mirror.

The chapters that follow provide new names for what we see if we look into that mirror—if we have the courage to look into it with fresh eyes.

CHAPTER 2

THE NEW PROVINCIALISM

The past is not dead. In fact, it's not even past.
—WILLIAM FAULKNER

In the middle third of the twentieth century, there was a flowering of literary productivity in the South. Called the Southern Literary Renaissance, it produced such figures as William Faulkner, Thomas Wolfe, Eudora Welty, Flannery O'Connor, Katherine Ann Porter, and Robert Penn Warren—the latter being a member of a group that came to be called the Fugitive-Agrarians. Scholars have spent the half century since the movement burned itself out trying to figure out what happened. They have said that these southerners had a strong sense of place. They have attributed their success as novelists to the tradition of southern storytelling. Some have said that the fact that the

South had been defeated in the Civil War gave southerners the sense of melancholy, a longing, perhaps even a guilt, that often produces great literature.

But for all the books written, none have been able to improve on Flannery O'Connor's assessment of the southern writer. To her friend Marion Montgomery in praise of his first novel, she wrote, "The Southern writer can outwrite anyone in the country because he has the Bible and a little history."[1]

This sense of history, this sense that the past is ever present in the consequences it produces, has always been a mark of civilized people. But this sense of history has been disdained by modernists. Before the first poems started coming from Robert Penn Warren and the other Fugitive poets in the 1920s, and books and stories started coming from Faulkner and Wolfe in the 1930s, H. L. Mencken was among those who had called the southern writers provincial and inconsequential—full of local color, perhaps, but lacking universal qualities.[2]

But some of the writers of the Southern Literary Renaissance fought back. One writer, in particular, defended the southern vision. Poet, critic, and editor Allen Tate, in a now-classic essay called "The New Provincialism," observed that the contemporary world—with its transportation and communication—allowed modernists to put on a cosmopolitan air.[3] The Internet might allow us to know, for example, what a celebrity had for breakfast, half-a-world away. But Tate argued that such knowledge had no value and no meaning. Today we might look with disdain on geographical provincialism. But we are trapped in a new provincialism of time. We are trapped in the ever-present now. We now live without a past or a future. We act with no regard to consequence. Effects admit no cause. The result is that we live in an age of ideology. We can make up any theory we like about how the world operates, and we look for data to support it.

Of course, the problem with the modernist's worldview is that it is sustainable only if time is erased. Because actions and ideas do have specific and related consequences, the only way we can keep our ideologies from crumbling under the weight of reality is to distort reality. The video media, which are dominant today, are particularly effective at this deconstruction of reality. When we fail to see that effects have causes because we have lost the ability to look clearly at history, we do not erase or eliminate these causes. But we do risk becoming victims of these corrosive causes again and again.

What I attempted to do in chapter one was to describe some of the effects. But these effects, the symptoms we discussed in chapter one—the seduction of evangelical leaders by political power and money—did not just appear ex nihilo. These symptoms have underlying pathologies. That's why it is important—if we are to understand what the modern evangelical church has become—that we recover, as Flannery O'Connor said, "the Bible and a little history."

So let's look at some of the great religious movements in U.S. history, movements to which our current age is often compared, and see if the comparisons hold up under scrutiny and if what is different about these religious movements helps us understand our present age.

The Great Awakening

The first of these great religious movements is a revival known by historians as the Great Awakening, or sometimes the First Great Awakening, which took place in the United States more or less between 1730 and 1745 and was typified by fiery but sober and generally unemotional preaching.

If Billy Graham is the archetypal figure of the modern evangelical movement, Jonathan Edwards, was the lion of the Great Awakening. He was famous for such sermons as "Sinners in the Hands of an Angry God." But those who saw him preach report that his style was anything but theatrical. "Sinners," in fact, was never extemporaneously delivered. Edwards often simply read it. Sometimes, when Edwards or another ordained clergyman could not be present at a service, it was read by a member of the congregation.

In a letter Edwards wrote in 1743 to his friend Thomas Prince, it is easy to see that what Edwards treasured among the gifts of the revival was not emotionalism, but the changed lives and improved communities where the revival took hold:

> There has been vastly more religion kept up in the town, among all sorts of persons, in religious exercises and in common conversation than used to be before. There has remained a more general seriousness and decency in attending the public worship. There has been a very great alteration among the youth of the town with respect to reveling, frolicking, profane and unclean conversation, and lewd songs. Instances of fornication have been very rare. There has also been a great alteration among both

old and young with respect to tavern haunting. I suppose the town has been in no measure so free of vice in these respects for any long time together for this sixty years as it has been this nine years past.[4]

Edwards was so concerned about fraudulent manifestations of religion and by criticisms of what he considered to be very real manifestations of God's power that in 1741 he wrote *The Distinguishing Marks of a Work of the Spirit of God.*

The fact that Edwards wrote it at all demonstrates that he believed, as Scripture commands, that we should test the spirit. (Some of today's evangelical preachers, by contrast, seem to believe that close scrutiny is a quenching of the Holy Spirit.) The details of that work are beyond the scope of our discussion, except to say this: Edwards, in *The Distinguishing Marks,* identified nine characteristics that do not prove there is a revival (one of which is "there is much talk about religion"). And he identified five characteristics that do indicate revival (one of which is that "men are led away from falsehood into truth").

In 1742, a year after Edwards wrote *The Distinguishing Marks,* he wrote another book defending the New England revival, saying that the great moral improvement of the country was evidence of true revival. Edwards famously asserted that in some towns where revival had occurred, taverns had closed and the poor had been helped to gainful employment.

There is no doubt that the impact of the Great Awakening was exactly that: great. Author David Barton, for example, believes that the American republic itself would not have been possible without the conviction of men who had their spiritual birth and nurturing in the Great Awakening.[5] S. E. Morison, in *The Oxford History of the American People*, speculated that less than a majority, only about 40 percent, of the white population in the colonies were Patriots, with about 50 percent indifferent or neutral. Around 10 percent were British Loyalists. However, among the Patriots were the religious leaders who had been shaped by the Great Awakening—Baptists and Presbyterians, primarily. Ashbel Green, the Presbyterian chaplain to Washington's Congress, wrote, "Many of those who took the lead in the arduous struggle which issued in the Independence of our country were . . . men of decided piety; and those of opposite character yielded to their influence, from a regard to popular opinion, which at that time was strongly in favor of religion."[6]

In other words, this Great Awakening—born of sober biblical preaching, a high regard for doctrinal purity, and a healthy skepticism of emotionalism—had an impact that bore fruit not in large crowds, but in transformative and permanent change in its culture, change that stood the test of time.

There are those who maintain that the flowering of evangelicalism since World War II is a great deal like this First Great Awakening. It is my contention, however, that what we are seeing today is much more like a very different religious phenomenon: the Second Great Awakening.

The Second Great Awakening

A second great religious movement swept the country around the year 1800 and brought with it the phenomenon of the camp meeting. The famous Cane Ridge, Kentucky, meetings of the summer of 1801 attracted as many as ten thousand people—that at a time when Lexington, Kentucky's largest city, had less than two thousand people.

News of the Cane Ridge meetings spread, though slowly, over the course of a decade or more, and others attempted to duplicate these revivals in format if not in result. Daylong meetings of fiery sermons, often with local drunks and notorious skeptics and doubters made to sit on benches near the speaker. Many succumbed to the public humiliation with genuine conviction and conversion. Others apparently professed conversion to be relieved of the front-row scrutiny—which at these revival meetings could go on for days.

These camp meetings resulted in large crowds and claims of many conversions to Christianity, but little positive social or cultural change followed. There were no tavern closings in the wake of this wildfire of revivalism, though many of the preachers themselves, including Charles Finney, the era's leading preacher, became celebrities. Instead, the lack of doctrinal depth of both the preachers and the converts caused many to turn away from faith and many more to go astray.

In short, the First Great Awakening resulted in churches that have remained faithful to gospel truth for nearly three centuries and in an experiment in liberty—the United States—that is a light to the world. The Second Great Awakening, on the other hand, created an environment in which cults such as the Jehovah's Witnesses and the Mormons could easily take root,[7] and by the end of the nineteenth century, many parts of the country that had experienced the Second Great Awakening were among the most irreligious, virtually inoculated to the preaching of the gospel. Finney himself left preaching to become president of Oberlin College. Many credit Finney with unmooring Oberlin from its Presbyterian roots. Today Oberlin is known for being perhaps the nation's most liberal and certainly the most gay-friendly college campus in the country.[8]

Post–World War II evangelicalism has been called the Third Great Awakening. And it may be just that. But will it bear lasting fruit as did the First Great Awakening? Or will it be remembered for a crass revivalism that enriched its leaders with money and power, but had no or little lasting impact on the kingdom of God like the Second Great Awakening?

This question—Will it result in lasting fruit?—is one of the themes of this book. But the reality is that we do not need to ask this question in the future tense. After a half century we should be asking: Has it borne lasting fruit?

Theological Fruit

There are, of course, a number of ways to answer this question. Because another theme of this book is the notion that ideas have consequences, let's look first at a couple of the big ideas that came out of the Second Great Awakening and attempt to evaluate the consequences of these ideas as they have manifested themselves in modern evangelicalism.

One of those ideas is what theologians call premillennialism. Because this is not a book about eschatology (the study of the end times), we will not dive too deeply into this murky pool. But a few basics are in order.

One of those basics is the idea that Christ will come again. This idea has always been a core belief of Christians of all stripes. Scripture has many references to Jesus' second coming, including some from Jesus himself. The idea that Christ will come again in glory to judge the living and the dead is part of the Nicene Creed of AD 325, which was an attempt to identify the essential beliefs of the Christian faith.

But when will he come? That question has divided Christians since the time of Jesus. Among the last words of the last Gospel arc these words from John 21:19–23:

> Then he [Jesus] said to him, "Follow me!"
>
> Peter turned and saw that the disciple whom Jesus loved was following them. . . . When Peter saw him, he asked, "Lord, what about him?"
>
> Jesus answered, "If I want him to remain alive until I return, what is that to you? You must follow me." Because of this, the rumor spread among the brothers that this disciple would not die. But Jesus did not say that he would not die; he only said, "If I want him to remain alive until I return, what is that to you?"

So even while Jesus was on earth, the date of his return was generating controversy among Christians. Jesus, though, said that no one knows the hour or the day (Matthew 24:36). And that is one of the reasons that the circumstances of Christ's return have historically been regarded by the church as a mystery. The liturgy of the Anglican, Roman, and Eastern churches, among others, states it this way in their respective masses: "This is the mystery of faith: Christ has died, Christ is risen, Christ will come again." That it will happen is an essential doctrine of the faith. How it will happen, it seems, is not for us to know.

But that hasn't stopped people from speculating and, in some cases, attempting to elevate that speculation to the level of settled doctrine. Historically, the Christian church has been amillennial. That is, the church has believed that the thousand-year reign referred to in Revelation 20 is symbolic and that the millennium is the same as the church age. This amillennial view seems to have been the dominant view of the preachers and theologians of the First Great Awakening.

However, in the aftermath of the Second Great Awakening, especially with the rise of the Seventh-day Adventist sect and such religions as Jehovah's Witnesses and the Mormons, a premillennial view developed. Premillennial views often developed in these new religions, or in churches that were either independent or had a congregational polity, outside the oversight and accountability of a larger Christian body and without historical theological precedents. They tended to be highly idiosyncratic. In other words, there is no "one-size-fits-all" description of premillennialism.

But, in general, the premillennial view holds that the millennium has not taken place. It will take place when Jesus returns. But first there will be a rapture of the church. This means that Christians will suddenly and supernaturally disappear from earth. This rapture is followed by a tribulation in which great hardship will occur for those left behind. During this time of tribulation many will come to faith, in part because the sudden and unexpected disappearance of hundreds of millions or even billions of Christians will convince many of a coming judgment. This remnant will stand against the Antichrist, who will emerge in this chaotic time. Jesus will return to lead this remnant in a final battle, which he and his followers will win, and Jesus will begin a thousand-year reign—the millennium—on earth.

If this brief description sounds familiar, it is because it is the dominant eschatological view of much of modern evangelicalism. But it is important to note that even though variations of premillennial views existed in sects from the early days of the church, the premillennial view was rejected by many of the early church fathers. Saint Augustine actively preached against the premillennial view in the fourth century. As I suggested above, the amillennial view has been the dominant view of the Roman, Anglican, and Eastern branches of Christendom, and it was also the dominant view of the Reformers and the Puritans.

This historical disdain for premillennialism by orthodox Christian theologians left premillennialism all but dead in the Christian church until it was resurrected in the nineteenth century. And cold-war America was fertile ground for the apocalyptic vision of premillenialism. In a very short time, it became the dominant eschatological view of modern evangelicalism, thanks partly to the rise of Dallas Theological Seminary, founded in 1924 in part to teach premillennialism.

Today most Baptists, including Southern Baptists, the nation's largest Protestant denomination, hold the view explicitly.[9] In 1970 premillennialism got a huge boost when Zondervan published a book by Hal Lindsey called *The Late Great Planet Earth*. The book sold over thirty million copies, is still in print, and is one of the best-selling religious books of all time. Lindsey himself, despite having many of his predictions fail to come to pass, remains a popular speaker in churches and on television.

The *Left Behind* books of the 1990s had, if possible, an even greater impact on evangelical thinking, in part because the authors of this series—Tim LaHaye and Jerry Jenkins—had been well established in evangelical circles long before the first *Left Behind* book was published in 1995. The *Left Behind* books remain brisk sellers even though they have now passed the thirty million mark. They have also spawned movies and video games.

This is a key point that we will develop more fully in the next chapter, but it is worth saying here: despite having a dubious biblical and historical ancestry, the premillennial view has become the dominant view of evangelical Christianity in large part because of the marketing power of large Christian publishers and broadcasters. Indeed, what is telling, you might even say damning, about the rise of premillennialism is not that so many evangelicals believe it, but that they had to reject the historical teachings of the church in order to do so. It may have been the first time—though it was not, as we shall see, the last time—that a doctrine came into widespread belief not because of its historical authenticity, but based almost exclusively on the power of the marketing machine behind it.

Indeed, premillennialism itself is not so dangerous a doctrine. Even most amillennialists will not call premillennialists heretics because these various eschatological views can be held without denying core Christian doctrine. The Roman Catholic Church, for example, does not condemn premillennialism but has stated that the doctrine "could not be taught safely."[10] This statement from the Catholic Church is one that neither affirms nor condemns. In fact, many theologians are agnostic on this issue, as they rightly should be on any issue called a mystery by the historical Christian church. What is dangerous is how quickly and easily the evangelical church is willing to jettison history and theology to embrace a doctrine that clearly has dubious roots and gets its sustenance in the materialism of modern culture.

In any case, our task here is not to condemn premillennialism, but to observe that it quite suddenly became a dominant view in the evangelical church. It is not clear that the rise of premillennialism was the cause or the result of the new provincialism; a case could be made for either. What is clear is that a hallmark of both is a disregard for the historical teachings of the Christian church.

It is also clear, too, that this premillennial view served well the kinds of evangelical efforts that became popular in the aftermath of the Second Great Awakening. Premillennialism, teaching, as it does, the possibility or even the probability of an imminent rapture, created the kind of urgency that brought people to a point of emotional crisis: "What if the rapture came . . . *now?!* Would I be left behind?"

Many "decisions" resulted from just such preaching.

The New Provincialism and the Incarnation

But how many true conversions resulted? Any discussion of the fruit of modern evangelicalism must, of course, deal with this issue. Now that forty years have passed since the Jesus Revolution of the 1960s and '70s and more than a half century has passed since the end of World War II and the flowering of the modern evangelical movement in the United States, it is obvious that only a fraction of the conversions touted by the megachurches, parachurches, and others could possibly have been valid.

In the 1970s and '80s, the Southern Baptist Convention faced accusations that some congregations were padding their membership rolls. The accusations turned out to be true, and in 1998 the denomination reported a 1 percent drop in membership, the first membership drop for the denomination in seventy years. Convention president Paige Patterson told the *New York Times*, "We've known for a long time the boasting numbers were inflated. Some of us were having a hard time with our consciences about it. Churches have been cleaning up their rolls, so I do not view the drop as unfortunate. We needed to get more honest about the numbers."[11]

This transparency and confession are welcome, but this acknowledgment is only an admission that a problem exists; it does not actually solve the problem. The core problem, this dislocation from history and causality that I am calling the new provincialism, is itself but a symptom of an evangelical theology that is slowly eroding the Christian view of the incarnation.

Let me explain what I mean by that.

The Christian faith is, if nothing else, a faith born in time. It depends on its history. God's covenants with people and Jesus' life, death, and resurrection are not merely ideas. They are historical events. Paul went so far as to say that if the resurrection is not a historical event, then our faith is in vain (1 Corinthians 15:17). In other words, when we reject the historicity of the faith, we come dangerously close to rejecting Jesus himself, for it is in history—the incarnation—and through Scripture that Jesus chose to reveal himself to us.

That is why it is so important to note this phenomenon of the evangelical church becoming an existential church, a church not bound by time and place. It has become, on the one hand, the church of the airwaves or, on the other hand, the megachurch—a place in which we gather for a very short time, but which we leave and, in some cases, travel long distances to get back to our homes. The modern evangelical church is most decidedly _not_ a church that is rooted in time and place. It is a church that desires to live outside of time, so to speak. Even the penchant of the evangelical church to target Gen-X populations or postmoderns—often to the exclusion of other age groups—is a manifestation of the new provincialism. Indeed, some megachurch pastors report that it has been many months since they have led a funeral service, because there are no old people in their churches.[12]

The most obvious, but in some ways the most superficial, indicator of the new provincialism in the modern evangelical church (or what we might more accurately call the modern existential church) is that it is almost impossible to find an evangelical church that is not contemporary in its worship. Let me simply observe here, to bring this part of our discussion to a close, that by the late 1960s the evangelical church had become a movement that had cut all ties with its past and—by then in the grips of premillennial thought—did not believe it had an earthly future. In 1971, *TIME* magazine put a psychedelic drawing of Jesus on its cover, with "The Jesus Revolution" as a headline. The article went on to recount a rootless youth culture, often engaged in communal living and street evangelism. Israel had become a nation in 1948, and Hal Lindsey's book popularized the notion that Jesus would return within a generation. Was a generation twenty years? Thirty years? Forty years? Certainly, no more than that. In this context the historical church and its theology were an impediment. Even disciple building, which should have been at the core of the Great Commission, seemed irrelevant.

The Overhead Church

By the mid-1970s everything about the evangelical movement had an aspect of the transient, the temporary, the ephemeral. The modern entertainment and celebrity culture, the one in which—as Andy Warhol said, "Everyone would be famous for fifteen minutes"—became not just a part of, but a hallmark of, the evangelical movement. Musicians, in particular, were highly prized trophies of what came to be called the Jesus People Movement. In the 1960s the song of choice of former hippies might have been "Kum Bah Ya." In the 1970s Larry Norman's premillennial ballad "I Wish We'd All Been Ready" replaced Luther's "A Mighty Fortress Is Our God" at the churches being started by these Jesus People alumni. By the 1990s worship music had become its own industry, prompting Christian music veteran Michael Card, someone who has been both a part of and a critic of the evangelical church and the Christian music industry, to ask, "When did worship stop being a sacrifice and start becoming a profit center?"[13]

Pierce Pettis is another Christian musician I interviewed for this book. I interviewed him in part because after many years in evangelical churches, he had converted to Roman Catholicism. He called the evangelical churches he attended before his conversion "overhead churches." Anyone who has attended an evangelical church knows exactly what he meant. Beginning in the 1970s, when evangelicals gathered, the focus of the congregation was not on an altar, a pulpit, a baptismal font, or a cross. The focus was, instead, on a big blank screen on which an overhead projector flashed announcements, song lyrics, and sermon notes. As technology evolved, the overhead was replaced by an LCD projector, a laptop, and PowerPoint. But the idea is the same. Hymnbooks and prayer books all but vanished from sanctuaries. Even Bibles became rare, since any Scripture needed as text for a sermon could be projected overhead. Indeed, sanctuaries all but vanished in favor of auditoriums with stadium-style seating.

Everything about these new churches, including their architecture, reflected the rootless, existential, modernist condition of the world. As we have suggested, even their reason for being—to target a specific age group—reflected a disdain for history. The activities and innovations of the evangelical church are fueled by pop culture, and youth culture in particular. These churches made no place for children and old people—and the joys, wisdom, and opportunities for service that they bring to the body of Christ. In fact, these churches, targeted as they were to a very narrow demographic, actively discouraged the kind of intergenerational community building that links us to history and, ultimately, to the eternal truths of the church.

In the end, the overhead church, whatever its particular manifestation, did not offer a refuge from or an antidote to our addiction to the modernist worldview.

Instead, it offered a fix.

What's Next?

It is tempting to dismiss these criticisms as being merely questions of style. However, if you have read this far, you can, I hope, clearly see that these issues are not merely questions of competing tastes or styles, but of competing worldviews and theologies. And the stakes are huge. At a minimum, the new provincialism that is now a dominant characteristic of the evangelical church has seriously compromised the witness of the Christian church in the world. At a maximum, the new provincialism has so dislocated us from history and biblical tradition that the evangelical church risks ceasing to be a Christian church at all.

This diagnosis may sound extreme. After all, not all headaches are caused by brain cancer.

True enough, but if two aspirins don't make the headache go away, further tests may be required. And that is where we are in our discussion. The new provincialism has dislocated us from our historical faith. As a result, doctrines that may not rise to the level of heresy, but are (at a minimum) historically irregular—such as premillennialism—have crept into the church. At this point, it seems unlikely that a denial of the incarnation of Christ could be next. But to many sincere preachers of the Second Great Awakening, it probably seemed unlikely that a significant fruit of that revival would be the existence of the Mormons and the Jehovah's Witnesses, which together claim twenty million members.

So let us not assume that the new provincialism is either benign or self-correcting. Let's look more deeply into the evangelical church that the new provincialism has helped to create and see what else there is to see.

CHAPTER 3

THE TRIUMPH OF SENTIMENTALITY

There is no corruption that threatens a country so surely as the sentimentalizing of its religion; and there is no corruption of the Christian religion so swift as that which sets in when the Church loses its strict Biblical discipline.

—E. C. HOSKYNS (1884–1937) IN *WE ARE THE PHARISEES*

We are susceptible to heretical teachings because, in one form or another, they nurture and reflect the way that we would have it be, rather than the way God has provided, which is infinitely better for us. As they lead us into the blind alleys of self-indulgence and escape from life, heresies pander to the most unworthy tendencies of the human heart.

—C. FITZSIMONS ALLISON IN *THE CRUELTY OF HERESY*

If you want to get anywheres in religion, you got to keep it sweet.

—HAZEL MOTES IN FLANNERY O'CONNOR'S *WISE BLOOD*

In the last chapter we made the point that the Christian God is one who chose to reveal himself to us in history. Because of that, when we forget history, to the extent of that forgetfulness, we worship a false god. In other words, the rejection of history—which I call the new provincialism—is in fact (again, to the extent of that forgetfulness) a denial of the incarnation. If we are to worship the one true God, we must worship not God as we would like him to be, but, as Francis Schaeffer said, as "the God Who Is There."

If we succumb to the new provincialism, what happens next? When we reject the God Who Is There and the history in which he revealed himself, we inevitably replace him with a god and a history of our own making. We create an alternate reality, which is actually not a creation of anything, but a deconstruction of reality. I call this deconstruction of objective reality and the construction of an alternate and subjective vision of the world the *triumph of sentimentality*.

This way of thinking about our modern malaise is not original to our discussion. Indeed, the first chapter of Richard Weaver's *Ideas Have Consequences*, the book on which this one depends much, is called "The Unsentimental Sentiment," and it brilliantly lays out the differences between reality and sentimentality. And this distinction between objective reality and its sentimental alternatives underpins even many evangelical writers, such as J. P. Moreland and Chuck Colson. Their position is that Christianity is the worldview that stands for objective reality, often called absolute truth by these evangelical writers.

The absolute truth of the Christian worldview stands against the attacks of hedonism, Darwinism, Marxism, materialism, and other "isms."

This critique, so far as it goes, is true. But the real question is this: Has evangelicalism become another "ism"? Is modern evangelicalism becoming just another alternate and subjective vision of the world?

In this chapter I want to reflect on that question. We will define more fully this triumph of sentimentality and contrast it with what Thomas Aquinas called "the truth of things." Further, we must be honest and clear-eyed about how today the evangelical church has followed the lead of the modernist by rejecting "the truth of things" and, either intentionally or not, attempted to create a past, present, and future that align not with how things are, but with how we would like them to be.

Utopias and Dystopias

This seductive power of sentimentality is not new. The longing to live in an ideal world or at least to better ourselves, to progress, is as old as humanity. The story of Eden gives us a glimpse of a perfect world, but it is interesting to note that the fall—Adam's original sin—was to believe that he could improve on the world God had given to him. The Serpent's temptation to Eve was a temptation to improve on Eden, to "be like God." This desire to "be like God," to assert our vision and dream of the world over the reality given us by God, is a powerful human urge.

So powerful, in fact, that it has become one of the great themes of literature. Plato's *Republic* and Augustine's *City of God* have been called examples of utopian literature. However, the word *utopia* was coined in 1516 by Sir Thomas More, who wrote of the imaginary island of Utopia, where people lived in harmony, free from poverty, tyranny, and war. But More, a devout Catholic who was ultimately martyred for his devotion to his faith, had no illusions that utopia could be achieved by humans. In fact, he exercised a bit of irony and subtlety in coining the word itself. *Utopia* is a combination of two Greek words: *eu*, meaning "good," and *topos*, meaning "land" or "place." In short, utopia is a "good place." But the word in Greek is a double entendre. *Ou* in Greek means "no." So the "good place" is also "no place." In other words, More's Utopia is not a place made by human hands.

Our most insightful modern writers have understood this reality, and their works have been not utopian, but dystopian. Writers such as George Orwell help us understand that when people attempt to implement their vision of a perfect future, the first step is to erase history, and the final outcome is tyranny and brutality.

Richard Weaver, in *Ideas Have Consequences*, argued that our senses and logical capabilities—what he called our "sentiment"—give us the ability to see and make sense of the order of the world, but not to make the world. According to Weaver, if the order that we see doesn't align with our desires, then our moral responsibility is to align our desires with the truth of things as they are. He called this ability to see the world as it is the "unsentimental sentiment."

So, on the one hand, humankind has the ability to see the order in the world, the world as it is. On the other hand, we also have an overpowering urge to reject the world as it is in favor of a world that we would prefer. This urge is "sentimentality." Sentimentality is the result of our unwillingness to realign our desires to the reality of the world, but rather to remake the world in accordance with our desires. Weaver attributed this impulse toward sentimentality as one of the primary causes of the decline of Western culture. "The defeat of logical realism in the great medieval debate was the crucial event in the history of Western culture," Weaver wrote. Weaver argued, as I am arguing, for a return to "logical realism" or, as one of his chapter titles puts it, a return to "the unsentimental sentiment."[1]

If these heady ideas seem irrelevant, or a mere intellectual indulgence, in our discussion of modern evangelicalism, it is only because Richard Weaver's prophecy has come fully to pass: we have lost the ability to connect the dots between ideas and their consequences. We have lost, for example, the ability to look at a book by megachurch pastor Joel Osteen and see that its very title offers the same promise as the Serpent offered Eve in the garden of Eden: *Your Best Life Now*! That Osteen could title his book thus, completely without irony, and that much of evangelicalism could accept it without criticism, are proof enough that these ideas are not irrelevant to modern evangelicalism.

But perhaps we can make these ideas a bit less abstract by looking at a particular seeker church and the lessons we can learn from its short, unhappy history.

Creating the "Nonchurch"

It was being billed around Charlotte, North Carolina, as "nonchurch," or "church for a postmodern generation." The offices for the church were in an artsy part of town in an old warehouse section that was rapidly undergoing gentrification. Thus the name of the new church: Warehouse 242.

The Reverend Todd Hahn, lead teaching pastor of Warehouse 242, had a goatee, a hip haircut, and an earring. He was quick to point out that his church was not some off-the-wall, renegade group. He was under the authority of the Evangelical Presbyterian Church (EPC). It's possible that even to those who follow denominational politics and permutations, the EPC might be either unknown or vaguely known; after all, there are so many Presbyterian denominations that even Presbyterians often refer to themselves as the "split peas." The EPC had a reputation as being the most contemporary and seeker oriented of the various Presbyterian denominations. There are several megachurches in the denomination, most famously the five-thousand-member Hope Presbyterian Church in suburban Memphis, Tennessee, where Christian music star Bruce Carroll was the minister of music. But both he and the denomination are "thoroughly Reformed," Hahn would say, a reference to the theology of the Reformation that had historically been the basis of Presbyterianism. "I'm a huge

Francis Schaeffer fan," he said. "Calvin. C. S. Lewis. Oh yeah. Huge fan."[2]

Even conceding that point, it would still be pretty hard to imagine Schaeffer, Calvin, or Lewis in the first Warehouse 242 service in September 1999. Though Hahn claimed that the service was designed for the unchurched, for those who "don't do church and have never done church," the crowd of over three hundred people who were at the first service was mostly young people from Warehouse 242's parent church, Forest Hill Church, a large EPC church in an affluent Charlotte suburb. Forest Hill used the same campus that Jim Bakker once used when he was a local pastor, before he went on to greater renown and ultimate disgrace at the PTL Club.[3]

The hard-rock music, video clips, and the Starbucks coffee shipped in for the services were carefully picked to appeal to the young urban professionals the church hoped to attract. As were the words used in the sermon. "No theological words," said Hahn, who has a seminary degree. "People who have never been to church just don't get that."

By 2001 the church had grown to more than seven hundred regular attenders,[4] and a veritable cult of personality had grown up around Todd Hahn. He was regularly interviewed by the mainstream media, and profiles of the church appeared on television and in the *Charlotte Observer*. The Willow Creek Association, born out of Willow Creek Community Church, the epicenter of the seeker movement, touted Hahn at its website and conferences. Hahn appeared in blue jeans on the cover of the *Christian Century* in early 2001.

All of this made what happened next an even bigger news story than it otherwise would have been, and—if possible—more tragic: on Sunday, December 9, 2001, Hahn was arrested on charges of simple assault, assault on a female (his wife), and making harassing phone calls.

Hahn and the other leaders in the church had eschewed the structure and accountability that come with more conventional church polity, so it was ironic when the next day Marc Dickmann, Warehouse 242's pastor of commitment, revealed that Hahn had been battling depression for more than a year. Dickmann added, "Those closest to Todd had those charges filed in order to allow him to receive the care that he needed. That may seem counterintuitive, but that was to keep Todd from harming himself."[5]

Part of the irony here, of course, is that this leadership team, which didn't want to do church in the conventional way, had no way of helping someone who, more than anything, needed what the church had historically provided: sanctuary, community, forgiveness, help, and healing. Instead, Hahn's increasingly pathological behavior was never checked by those around him, and when it got out of control, those around him had no recourse other than to call the police.

It is, of course, unfair to blame what happened at Warehouse 242 on the seeker model. This kind of thing happens in traditional churches too. But it is not at all unfair to observe that human beings, even those who are attempting to be on their best behavior, are still human beings. Any church structure that is not designed to account for the inevitability that human beings will act like human beings is to that extent pathological. So while traditional church structure and denominationalism itself have their share of critics and some inherent limitations, they at least acknowledge this reality: people are born in sin. Leaders, even Christian leaders, require checks and balances in their lives. Accountability and community are essential conditions of health for both the individual Christian and the church as a whole.

So, the question before us is whether Warehouse 242 is an anomaly or an inevitability. Before we answer that question, it's important to note that Warehouse 242 is most definitely not an anomaly in the world of evangelicalism. The number of so-called seeker or emergent churches is hard to pin down, but the Willow Creek Association claims more than twelve thousand member churches on its website (www.willowcreek.com/AboutUs). Clearly, it is a significant and growing movement, so it would perhaps be helpful to look at the church that is widely considered to be ground zero for the movement.

Willow Creek Community Church

Willow Creek Community Church and its dynamic pastor, Bill Hybels, are in many ways strategically located to have an impact on the entire nation. Being, as it is, in the Chicago suburb of South Barrington, Illinois, it is not only in the third largest city in the United States but also near some of the most influential Christian ministries and colleges in the country, including Wheaton College and the Moody Bible Institute. And South Barrington is the kind of edge city or exurb that has driven economic growth in the country in the last quarter of the twentieth century. In other words, it is one of the most affluent, fastest-growing, and whitest U.S. towns.[6] In many ways, South Barrington is what America aspires to be.

Today Willow Creek Community Church is also what many churches aspire to be. It is the archetype of the modern evangelical megachurch. In 2005 the church claimed 21,500 members, making it the sixth largest Protestant congregation in the United States.[7] But these days, being big is not really a distinguishing characteristic. You must be not merely big but really big to have credibility with other church-growth mavens. Of the one hundred largest churches in the United States in 2004, all had well surpassed the two-thousand-member mark of the mere megachurch and were beginning to be called supermega by some who study the phenomenon. And almost all of the churches on the list were less than fifty years old. Mars Hill Bible Church, in Grandville, Michigan, pastored by Rob Bell, claimed ten thousand members by its fifth year of existence.[8]

What distinguishes Willow Creek is that it rises to the top in all the categories that the church-growth movement prizes—size, speed of growth, and influence on other churches. That it is large is self-evident. But it has risen to its exalted place on the list of the largest in less than twenty years, and it continues to grow. Further, by creating the Willow Creek Association, it has mentored others in its strategies and techniques for church growth.

Willow Creek, like so many megachurches and parachurch organizations, was born out of youth ministry—in this case, the youth ministry of another suburban Chicago church called

South Park Church, in the nearby suburb of Park Ridge. South Park Church itself was no mainline, old-school church. Though the mother of Willow Creek Community Church, it is barely an adolescent itself. Founded in 1947, South Park was also a non-denominational, evangelical church. In 1972 Bill Hybels began leading a youth group there. The group called itself "Son Life," and within a year the group had nearly tripled in size on the strength of Hybels's personality and teaching and the style of the meetings themselves, which included the early '70s equivalent of praise and worship songs.

But Hybels has said that a group needs a mission, and in May 1973 Son Life was intentionally reengineered as an outreach to nonbelieving youth. Hybels saw the move as a way to continue to interest the youth who were already there, to give them—and not just the leadership of the group—a mission. It was also the only way to continue the growth, since by then virtually every young person who was a member of the church was already involved in the youth group.

This decision may seem logical and well intentioned to us today. Indeed, many youth groups are considered outreaches of the church, not intended, or at least not primarily intended, for spiritual formation or discipleship. But that only shows the extent to which the Willow Creek model has become the dominant model of American evangelicalism. In fact, Hybels's decision to reach out to unchurched people and not "dig down" with current members and in turn help them become soul winners and disciple makers in their own families was a turning point for Hybels, according to G. A.

Pritchard, who wrote a critical history of the Willow Creek movement.[9]

It was also a turning point in evangelicalism. One of the unintended consequences of a church that is constantly focused more on outreach than spiritual formation is that this model all but ensures that every generation would have to be reevangelized, since the current adult generation does not have the spiritual training or maturity to raise its own children in the nurture and admonition of the Lord.

Pritchard's *Willow Creek Seeker Services,* despite this and many other criticisms, offers a straightforward history of the Willow Creek movement. And Pritchard is careful to say that none of these consequences were engineered out of malice or a desire for celebrity or empire. They were truly the unintended consequences of young men and women who were doing the best they could. And the reengineered Son Life grew rapidly, seducing these young leaders into believing that God was blessing their efforts. By 1975 Son Life had grown to more than a thousand young people, far more people than South Park Church had at that time. Indeed, the large group was no longer meeting at the church, having outgrown it, and some of the people attending had "aged out" of the original youth group, but they kept coming anyway and bringing their friends.

So in 1975, the leadership of Son Life decided to implement the same "principles on an adult level by starting a church," wrote Don Cousins, one of the organizers of the church.[10] According to Cousins, Hybels, and others who were there, most of the staff of the new church came from the staff of the youth group. This was an intentional decision. Because they were creating a new kind of church, there was a belief that they had to grow their staff from within, as those coming in from traditional church structures outside of Willow Creek wouldn't "get it." This was another vital and defining decision. Because Hybels had little formal theological education and because the church recruited most of the leadership from the youth group, another unintended consequence was virtually guaranteed: the spiritual maturity of the new leadership would rise to the level of the maturity of the current leadership, but could likely rise no further. That would be fine if the church had somehow stumbled on a method or process for disciple making and spiritual formation heretofore unknown or lost somewhere in the history of the church. But it was a risky and presumptuous decision.

It's likely, though, that the young leadership of the church understood neither the risk nor the presumption of the decision. Don Cousins, for example, defended the decision. "It is extremely difficult to judge a person's character or spiritual authenticity in an interview. You have to see them at work for some time." For this reason, Pritchard said, "Willow Creek does not like to hire individuals who haven't demonstrated their character there."[11]

The legacy of this history and this decision to recruit from within is both positive and negative. Over the years, Willow Creek has seen stability among its senior leadership team that is uncommon and that most people would judge to be positive. Pritchard said that during the time he studied Willow Creek, Hybels supervised three individuals in a management team who in turn managed the rest of the staff. Two of these three were students in the original thirty-member youth group.

But the other side of that coin is that it leaves one man—Bill Hybels—in firm control. Pritchard wrote, "Virtually all the church's work has remained firmly in the hands of people who shared the common experience of the youth group."[12] A related consequence is that despite the fact that Willow Creek has gotten bigger and older, it remains essentially, in methodology and content, a youth group. Mike Breaux, who was a teaching pastor at Willow Creek, is not bashful to admit that. He said what he does is "youth ministry for big people."[13]

Because Willow Creek is so intentionally youth ministry for big people, entertainment—or infotainment—is at the center of the church's methodology. The founder of the youth ministry Young Life, Jim Rayburn, famously said, "It's a sin to bore a kid with the gospel."[14] Willow Creek takes this admonition seriously, filling its sermons with drama and music, all strongly supported by state-of-the-art audiovisual accoutrement. Something is always happening on stage. And that activity is designed specifically to help "nonchurched Harry"—as Hybels often describes the generic seeker—see that church and Christianity are not boring. Pritchard quoted Hybels from one of the many pastors' conferences that Willow Creek gives through its Willow Creek Association: "Variety, variety, variety, variety. You'll get sick of hearing that in the next couple days. But friends, in every other environment except church, nonchurched Harry is exposed to variety."[15]

That nonchurched Harry might be coming to church to encounter something permanent and unchanging is a point lost here. That the church should be offering something permanent and unchanging, regardless of whether nonchurched Harry wants it or not, is doubly lost.

Downstream from Willow Creek

All creeks eventually run to the sea, so it is instructive to look downstream of Willow Creek to see if what it's putting in the water is adding to the refreshment or making the river water unfit to drink.

Pritchard used a similar metaphor in summing up the Willow Creek phenomenon. He wrote:

> Imagine Hybels and his team attempting to save someone being swept down a swiftly moving river. Hybels reaches out to try to catch the unfortunate soul before he or she is swept away. Hybels is using the tools of our culture to reach out to the unchurched Harrys being swept away to the judgment. Yet in attempting to reach out to others in the fast-flowing river of our culture, Hybels and his followers also sometimes fall in.[16]

The roots of Willow Creek Community Church in youth work are particularly instructive for anyone trying to identify what has become the dominant gene in the evangelical movement.

And this should be no surprise either. For nearby is Wheaton College. If any place can be called ground zero of the American evangelical movement, it is Wheaton. The college, founded in

1860, had its roots in the Second Great Awakening. Its first president, Jonathan Blanchard, had ties to Charles Finney's Oberlin College. Academically, it was a cut above average, but not so much above that it could be counted among such elite colleges as Harvard, Yale, and Princeton. Almost immediately after its founding, the school lost over half of its student body to service in the Civil War. But the school sent them away with pride, as President Blanchard was a well-known abolitionist and social reformer.

It was not until the third decade of the twentieth century that Wheaton College became what it would ultimately be known for: a stalwart of conservative and evangelical theology that also maintained high academic standards. When James Oliver Buswell became president of the college in 1925, the so-called higher criticism was inflicting itself on the academy. Higher criticism, which turned the study of theology into an amalgam of sociology, linguistics, and psychology, had already taken over most secular college religion departments and even many church-sponsored colleges.

In the early part of the twentieth century, in response to this takeover of religion departments by liberal theology, many new colleges were created by religious fundamentalists and conservative denominations.[17] Bob Jones University, for example, was founded in 1927. Billy Graham briefly attended this school, which went on to become the nation's most famous bastion of fundamentalism. William Jennings Bryan, the great lawyer and orator, who argued for the Bible at the famous Scopes Monkey Trial in Dayton, Tennessee, died days after the completion of that trial. In his honor, and on the strength of publicity generated by this trial that put "God in the dock" for all to see, the Bryan Memorial University Association launched a national campaign to raise $5 million, an enormous sum in those days, half for endowment and half for buildings. Classes began there—at what is today Bryan College—in 1930.

But Wheaton College was of a different stripe. It was not founded out of reactionary tendencies, as were these colleges, but it did have to react, to make a choice. And under Buswell's leadership, it took a conservative turn. In the 1930s, '40s, and '50s, Wheaton was one of the few colleges in the country that could offer a strong academic heritage as well as clear, conservative, biblically based distinctives. It attracted young men intent on Christian service but who fancied themselves more in tune with the times than the fundamentalists. Billy Graham's own journey was typical. Unhappy at Bob Jones University, this son of the South came north to Wheaton. One of his classmates was Carl Henry, who with Graham founded *Christianity Today* magazine. Moody Bible Institute was nearby. Chicago's Pacific Garden Mission and its pioneering radio program, *Unshackled*, were often staffed by Wheaton students and recent graduates.

What was common to all of these activities and organizations was a commitment to evangelical theology and a willingness to use the media and modern methods to communicate the ancient truths of the gospel. It was out of this milieu that Willow Creek Community Church was founded and in which it grew. Indeed, it was a Wheaton College professor, Gilbert Bilezikian, who is often called the theologian of Willow Creek. Bilezikian was on a two-year teaching assignment at Trinity Evangelical Divinity School in Evanston, Illinois, when a young Bill Hybels came into his classroom in 1975. Hybels was deeply influenced by the Wheaton professor, and the young man would ride his motorcycle to Wheaton to get advice from his former professor. In fact, it was on Bilezikian's lawn one afternoon that Hybels said, "Dr. B., you and I are going to start a church."[18] That church, founded in a movie theater, became Willow Creek Community Church.

The rise of Willow Creek Community Church has been so recent and so public that there is no need to fully document it here. For now, it is enough to say that it has spawned thousands of imitators, including Todd Hahn's Warehouse 242, the church we mentioned at the beginning of the chapter and one that is a member of the Willow Creek Association—an organization that charges thousands of churches several hundred dollars a year to gain access to the latest thinking and material from Hybels and his staff.

Whatever the secrets of the success of Willow Creek and its offspring, adherence to biblical theology appears to be optional. While the Willow Creek Association itself has a biblical doctrinal statement, it does not require its members to adhere to the statement. Indeed, with twelve-thousand member churches from ninety denominations, a common doctrine would be impossible to identify or enforce.

And if there is a single church in the country that exemplifies the Willow Creek model perhaps even better than Willow Creek itself, it is one of the Willow Creek Association's earliest member churches: Houston's Lakewood Church.

Positively Dangerous

One of the hallmarks of churches in the Willow Creek mold is that they—in the words of a Broadway lyric—"accentuate the positive." And no preacher on the modern scene has been relentlessly more positive than Lakewood's pastor, Joel Osteen.[19]

Joel Osteen is upbeat, and if you believe his press clippings, he has much to be upbeat about. He became, to use the words of Dr. Norman Geisler, the "flavor of the week" in 2004 with the publication of his book *Your Best Life Now: 7 Steps to Living at Your Full Potential.* The book shot to the top of the secular and Christian bestseller lists. It became a fixture on the notoriously difficult-to-crack *New York Times* bestseller list because of 1.5 million hardback sales during the first year of publication. And his power-of-positive-thinking message has made the church he pastors, Houston's Lakewood Church, number one on *Outreach* magazine's 2005 list of largest churches in the nation, with more than thirty-two thousand people coming to hear him preach live each Sunday. Amazingly, it was also number three on the fastest-growing list, adding three thousand members in a single year.[20]

Osteen's perpetual optimism and populist appeal have made him one of the rising stars of both the charismatic movement and the church-growth movement. But critics have arisen as fast as the ministry itself. One critic is Robert Liichow, the founder of Discernment Ministry International, a Detroit-based apologetics ministry that examines and critiques ministries like Osteen's. Liichow said the same optimism and appeal that draw hundreds of thousands of people to Osteen's church and preaching events each year may also draw many of the same people away from the whole truth of the Bible.[21]

Critics like Liichow say that Osteen, by preaching nearly exclusively about human potential and the goodness of God, presents a deficient gospel, devoid of its most essential components: the sinfulness of humanity and the holiness of God and, therefore, our essential need for the redemption offered in Christ.

Michael Horton of Westminster Seminary California said that Osteen and others in the Willow Creek/megachurch movement would deny this charge. "It's not their stated theology," Horton said. "If you asked them questions of doctrine, they would likely give you the right answers. But it's their operational theology. Willow Creek, Joel Osteen, and others who have adopted this ministry model didn't create the modern American culture of consumerism, but they have not resisted it, and in many ways have explicitly adopted it. They treat people as consumers who need to be satisfied, and not as sinners who need to be justified."[22]

Lakewood Church has become the archetype of this model. It was founded in 1959 by Osteen's father, John Osteen. John was originally a Southern Baptist pastor but left the denomination when he began preaching charismatic and "word of faith" theology. Under his leadership the church soon grew to megachurch status. His son Joel briefly attended Oral Roberts University, but he soon dropped out to return to Houston and work in the

audiovisual ministry of the church. When John Osteen died unexpectedly of a heart attack in 1999, Joel took over the church.

But Osteen's gifts of organization and his experience running the media ministry of the church, which included a weekly
television broadcast, soon became apparent. Joel Osteen's tele-
genic good looks and his relentlessly positive message—even in
the face of his father's death—touched an emotional chord with
people. Though Lakewood had six thousand members when he
took over, it immediately started growing again. Soon after taking
the helm, Osteen negotiated a deal with the city of Houston to
lease and renovate the Compaq Center, a sixteen-thousand-seat
arena and former home of the Houston Rockets. The church
ultimately invested a reported $92 million in renovations and
$12.3 million for a thirty-year lease for its new home.

For those who can't or don't want to join the crowds on
Sundays, Lakewood broadcasts its services in dozens of television
markets, reaching 95 percent of U.S. households with cable, as
well as tens of thousands more viewers in 150 countries. Some
years the program gained the number one spot in Nielsen's ratings of inspirational television shows.

Osteen takes the show on the road more than a dozen times
a year, selling out the largest arenas in major U.S. cities, including New York City's Madison Square Garden twice.

But as Osteen's ministry became more prominent, the gaps
in his theological education became apparent. Criticism from
evangelical theologicans intensified after an interview on *Larry
King Live*, when Osteen refused to say that Jesus is the only way
to heaven:

KING: What if you're Jewish or Muslim, you don't accept Christ at all?

OSTEEN: You know, I'm very careful about saying who would and wouldn't go to heaven. I don't know.

KING: If you believe you have to believe in Christ? They're wrong, aren't they?

OSTEEN: Well, I don't know if I believe they're wrong. I believe here's what the Bible teaches and from the Christian faith this is what I believe. But I just think that only God will judge a person's heart. I spent a lot of time in India with my father. I don't know all about their religion. But I know they love God. And I don't know. I've seen their sincerity. So I don't know. I know for me, and what the Bible teaches, I want to have a relationship with Jesus.[23]

Some said that Larry King, who had interviewed Billy Graham just weeks before, seemed to have a more complete understanding of the gospel than Osteen. In fairness to Osteen, he appeared on *Larry King Live* a year later and clarified his earlier statements, saying that he liked to focus on "God's goodness" and not on "man's sin."

But it is precisely this emphasis that has caused such theologians as Albert Mohler to say Osteen is a "pandering prophet."[24]

But the pandering seems to be working, as the growth of the church indicates. Osteen seems to think so. "I think Joel views the fact that Lakewood is the largest church in America as a sign of God's favor," said Liichow. "But Mormonism is one of the fastest-growing religious groups in America, and Islam is one of the fastest-growing religions in the world. We certainly can't say that's a sign of God's favor."

Instead of numbers, Liichow said Christians should examine content. And it is Osteen's content that troubles critics like Liichow. The basic message of *Your Best Life Now: 7 Steps to Living at Your Full Potential* is how to achieve happiness by getting what you want and developing your full potential. Osteen defines happiness and success in terms of earthly blessings: a better job, a better house, a stronger marriage, better health, a good parking spot at a crowded mall. The reader begins to ask, How can I get all these things? Osteen provides an answer: positive thinking.

"To experience this immeasurable favor," Osteen writes, "you must rid yourself of that small-minded thinking and start expecting God's blessings. . . . You must make room for increase in your own thinking, then God will bring those things to pass."[25]

Osteen calls this method "declaring God's favor" and says that it will work even in the most mundane circumstances. For example, if you find yourself in a crowded restaurant and you're in a hurry, Osteen suggests saying: "Father, I thank You that I have favor with this hostess and she's going to seat me soon."[26]

Osteen's focus on personal prosperity overshadows any talk of personal piety in a biblical context. In fact, the average bookstore browsers who pick up Osteen's work won't likely realize they are looking at a "Christian" book, at first glance.

Osteen acknowledges that the book's title and subtitle are devoid of Christian language and says there's a good reason. "I don't want to just preach to the church, and I just feel like I have a broader message," Osteen told Beliefnet.com. "I'd like to think I can help everyday people who don't necessarily go to church."[27]

Curiously, though, it isn't just the book's title and subtitle that are devoid of the biblical language of the gospel. The rest of the book is largely devoid of such content as well. Osteen makes no real mention of the unbeliever's problem of sin or the provision of salvation in Christ or of the believer's ongoing struggle with sin. While on the last page Osteen offers a three-sentence prayer for becoming a Christian, he offers no explanation of what salvation really means.

In fact, Osteen apparently doesn't insist a person must be a Christian in order to apply the principles in his book. FaithfulReader.com posed this question to Osteen: "Do you need to have a personal relationship with Christ or even be a Christian in order to benefit from what you write?" Osteen replied: "I think these principles will work in anybody's life."[28] Playing up happiness and downplaying sin are calculated moves, according to Osteen. "I just don't believe in condemning people and being judgmental," he continued. "It's the goodness of God that leads to repentance."

Liichow said that Osteen, by admittedly downplaying half of the gospel message and focusing on the pursuit of God's gifts instead of God himself, is putting both Christians and non-Christians in serious danger.

Michael Horton agreed. "God is not the center of his theology," said Horton. "The center is me and my happiness."

Horton said Osteen "trivializes the Christian faith" on a number of levels. "First, he trivializes God by making him out to be some sort of cosmic bellhop, as if God exists for us instead of us existing for him," says Horton. "Secondly, he trivializes the Bible by turning it into a collection of fortune cookies to be opened and used for whatever we want. And thirdly, he trivializes human beings and their real problems by trivializing sin."

Horton likened Osteen's feel-good, sugar-sweet theology to cotton candy. "Cotton candy won't kill you if you eat it a couple of times a year, but if you make it the only thing in your diet it will kill you," he said. "It won't just stunt your growth; it will kill your growth."

Liichow agreed, except he compared Osteen's theology to Twinkies. "The biggest danger for believers who listen to Osteen is that they will not grow in their spiritual life with the Lord Jesus Christ," said Liichow. "It's like eating spiritual Twinkies. They're sweet, light, and taste good; but a steady diet of them will rot you from the inside out."

But Osteen's theology isn't just dangerous for Christians, according to Liichow and Horton. It's also dangerous for unbelievers who may never hear the whole gospel by listening to Osteen. According to Liichow, "The danger for unbelievers is that they will never come to a genuine saving faith because they are never going to hear the full gospel—that they are totally depraved people without any hope in this world apart from Christ. I don't hear Joel preaching that.

"He's basically telling people: 'You're okay, but you could do so much better with Jesus,'" Liichow continued. "But that's not the truth. People are not okay. They are sinners in need of redemption."

Osteen's critics say there is nothing wrong with temporal prosperity, but that the Bible emphasizes spiritual joys over earthly ones. "The only thing we can look to in order to know whether or not we are truly prospering is Christ," said Horton. "The abundant life Jesus said he came to give is himself."

Liichow agreed. "It's true that God wants us to live an abundant life. We're called to have an abundant spiritual relationship with the Lord and to store up treasures in heaven. That's not the message Osteen's followers hear. I'm not saying that God couldn't use Osteen's preaching to convert someone because conversion is a work of the Holy Spirit. The Bible says God does use the foolishness of preaching. But I just don't know how much he uses foolish preaching. And there is a difference."

Damning with Faint Praise

There are a number of fair questions or rebuttals a careful reader could pose regarding this criticism of Todd Hahn at Warehouse 242, Bill Hybels at Willow Creek Community Church, and Joel Osteen at Lakewood Church.

First of all, you could ask a fundamental question: Are any of these three guilty of anything resembling heresy? Todd Hahn ended up getting put in an elevated position too quickly, and he crashed and burned. Osteen lacks seminary training, but is anything he is saying actually heretical? None of the men or the churches they lead are denying the divinity of Christ or the physical resurrection of Jesus or any other doctrine that might be considered essential. Hahn, Hybels, and Osteen are people with good intentions or, at least, people whose intentions we have no valid reason to question. Why pick on them?

A partial answer to this question is that our concern here is to understand how modern evangelicalism is resulting in a church that is getting sicker and smaller. It's true that writers such as Christopher Hitchens and Richard Dawkins, whose books touting atheism have been bestsellers, have attempted a full-frontal assault against Christianity. But it is also true that, for the most part, the evangelical church has been immune to these assaults. No evangelical pastor has said, "I just read Hitchens's *God Is Not Great*, and I have renounced my faith. He convinced me. God is *not* great."

But apparently many evangelical pastors who have read Bill Hybels have come to believe that preaching and sacraments are not enough. This despite the fact that these are the methods given to us by Jesus and Scripture. In other words, evangelicals have enough of a theological legacy still intact to reject the notion that God is not great. But we are no longer able to stand against the notion that God is not sovereign or that God is not sufficient. These notions are what Michael Horton has called the "operational theology" of the Willow Creek and seeker churches, even if they are not the explicitly stated theology of these churches.

Another question careful readers might reasonably ask is why we would put all of these churches in the same category. Joel Osteen's clearly charismatic/Pentecostal leanings are very different from the mainstream evangelicalism of Bill Hybels and Willow Creek. And Warehouse 242, despite the way it looks from the outside, claims to adhere to the same Reformed tradition that was birthed by John Calvin.

But they share an important—an overriding—characteristic in common. In the last chapter we examined how a new provincialism among evangelicals has made them a people with neither past nor future, thereby liberating evangelicals from having to take responsibility for the consequences of their actions and ideas. To this new provincialism we can add another expression to our descriptors of American evangelicalism: a triumph of sentimentality.

The Triumph of Sentimentality

You will remember in the last chapter we said that the new provincialism is the result of a flawed or incomplete view of history. It is a view of the world that perhaps unwittingly, but nonetheless thoroughly, rejects the historicity of the Christian faith. A failure to regard the consequences of ideas as they show themselves over time is, in fact, a denial of a God who works in history, who—in his wisdom and sovereignty—chose the incarnation, which is an intervention in history, as his way of redeeming the world.

Sentimentality, as we said early in this chapter, is a false notion of the world as it is. Sentimentality is the world as we would like it to be. Joel Osteen, for example, wants to emphasize God's goodness and his mercy but not God's holiness and his justice or our sinfulness. He is not alone in what Michael Horton called a "one-sided, reductionistic" theology. The Willow Creek seeker model likewise provides a limited definition of God. The very idea of a seeker is, according to Horton, theologically suspect. "Scripture teaches that no one seeks after God," Horton said. "Even our halting impulses toward God are born of his grace, not our spiritual desires."

All of this is why the sentimentality of the evangelical movement is so dangerous. These qualities of God—holiness and justice, mercy and wrath—cannot be separated one from the other. It is true that God is infinite, that we are finite, and that humans are therefore never able to fully discern the complete glory and character of God. There are mysteries of God that will not be known because they cannot be known.

But it is also true that humankind is the pinnacle of God's creative handiwork and that we can and should discern all of what God intends for us to discern of his character.

That is why the sentimentality of the evangelical church is idolatry, because it replaces a biblical God with one we prefer. This new god is therapeutic, but not redemptive. By embracing this new god made in our own image, we commit the same sin Eve committed in the garden of Eden: "You will be like God."

That's why it is ultimately inadequate to ask and answer the questions about Osteen, Bill Hybels and the megachurch movement, the emergent church movement, and other modern manifestations of sentimentality by simply looking at their doctrinal statements. What is or is not in the doctrinal statements of most parachurch ministries or independent, nondenominational churches is almost the least of our concerns. James was trying to tell us this when he said, "You believe that there is one God. Good! Even the demons believe that—and shudder" (James 2:19). James was trying to make us understand that faith without works is dead. He wanted us to see that we show our faith by our works. It is not too much of a hermeneutical stretch to say this: *We show our acceptance of the gospel when we behave in ways that show our submission to God's ordering of the universe and when we reject our view of the world and pursue God's mind in all matters.*

We don't talk much about sentimentality as idolatry, in part because sentimentality has pervaded every area of our lives. And it must be confessed that neither Joel Osteen nor Willow Creek nor emergent church leaders created this condition. "You can't blame this on Willow Creek," Michael Horton said. "They're a symptom, not a cause. It's increasingly difficult to swim against the tide of the culture's materialism, consumerism, and narcissism."

But sentimentality is idolatry, if idolatry is worshiping any god other than (as we described him to begin this chapter) the God Who Is There. Any god who is not sovereign or sufficient is just as false as one who is "not great," as Christopher Hitchens believes.

Nonetheless, it must also be confessed that we are at a point in history when to reject sentimentality (a false and *dis*-integrated view of God and the world) would be to essentially blow up modern evangelicalism and start over, something none or few of us are prepared to do. That's why we tend to give a pass to ourselves and to our popular televangelists when they succumb to sentimentality.

This idea is at the heart of Richard Weaver's *Ideas Have Consequences*, and it is why he called the first chapter of that little book "The Unsentimental Sentiment." Weaver's concerns were not so much religious in nature, but he was concerned with the destructive power of a *dis*-integrated worldview, a worldview that is not organic and coherent. He summed things up this way: "Whether we describe this as decay of religion or loss of interest in metaphysics, the result is the same; for both are centers with no power to integrate, and, if they give way, there begins a dispersion which never ends until the culture lies in fragments."[29]

My concern is not so much that the culture lies in fragments, but for the church—the bride of Christ, for whom he died and for whom he begged for unity, oneness (John 17:20–23).

So, you see, this is not a matter of hairsplitting over the fine points of doctrine. This is not a debate about how many angels can dance on the head of a pin. These questions ultimately go to the character of God, the efficacy of Jesus as Redeemer, and the power, authority, and influence of the gospel in the world—the only power for salvation.

So what is the antidote to the sentimentality—and, to hearken back to chapter one, the provincialism—that has all but poisoned our evangelicalism? The short answer—too short, at least for this stage in our discovery—is vocation and community, ideas that we will explore more fully in chapter eight.

But before we say too much more about that, let's continue our diagnosis of the current malaise and turn our attention to an aspect of evangelicalism where some of the ideas we have discussed can be seen in full voice. It's a phenomenon I call the Christian-industrial complex.

CHAPTER 4

THE CHRISTIAN-INDUSTRIAL COMPLEX

The merchant can please God only with difficulty.
—SAINT JEROME

In his farewell address to the nation, Dwight Eisenhower gave a speech that became famous because it used the expression *military-industrial complex*. Eisenhower said, "A vital element in keeping the peace is our military establishment. Our arms must be mighty, ready for instant action, so that no potential aggressor may be tempted to risk his own destruction." But Eisenhower warned of great danger if the military preparedness of our nation came to be seen as a market of private industrial interests. Eisenhower did not fear that military men would seek war, because whatever attractions war may have to a certain kind of soldier, Eisenhower knew that soldiers ultimately paid the price demanded by war with their lives. But he feared that leaders of industry would have no such check on their baser instincts. They could reap the benefits of war without having to pay the price of war. Eisenhower viewed the relationship between the military and industry as not merely symbiotic, but parasitic and pathological.

I use this historical example so that it might be easier to see that a similar pathological relationship has emerged between the Christian retail industry and the Christian church, which I call the *Christian-industrial complex.*[1] In chapter one we saw some of the ways the church has been co-opted by the Christian conference industry. But the Christian meeting and conference industry is just a small part of the rapidly expanding Christian-industrial complex, as we will now see.

The Christian Retail Industry

The headline on the Sunday, November 28, 2004, *New York Times* article was typically understated. Rachel Dondio's piece was titled simply "Faith Based Publishing."

When Joel C. Rosenberg read Dondio's article, he laughed. Rosenberg described himself as a "nice Jewish boy" whose life had "crashed into Jesus" a few years earlier. He was also one of the rising stars of faith-based publishing. His novel *The Last Jihad* is a thriller about an openly evangelical president facing a terrorist threat. It has a ripped-from-the-headlines, potboiler feel that caused critics to hate it.

But Rosenberg is hard-wired to thought leaders in the conservative and Christian world, and he is a brilliant public relations strategist, having worked for several conservative U.S. politicians as well as some Israeli politicians, including Prime Minister Ariel Sharon. Because the book has openly Christian characters, WORLD, the nation's largest weekly Christian news magazine (for whom Rosenberg served as a Washington correspondent) put the book and its young author on its cover. Rush Limbaugh started pumping the book to his fifteen million weekly listeners. That week, it hit the *New York Times* bestseller list, forcing Rosenberg to take an extended leave of absence from his post as a correspondent. The leave of absence was to handle all the new public appearance requests and to write another novel, which his publisher wanted as soon as possible and who was willing to give him a significant advance to get his undivided attention. As Rosenberg said, "So much for the day job."

But Rosenberg remained a popular blogger, and when the *Times* story hit, he wrote, "Lo and behold, Christians can read. Not only that, they buy books. Lots of them. Who woulda thunk it?"[2]

Rosenberg knew the answer to that question: millions of people. That the Christian market is huge and getting bigger, growing faster than all other publishing niches, is America's worst-kept secret, a mystery—Rosenberg suggested—only to sophisticates in "blue states" who read the *New York Times*.

Indeed, the numbers are astonishing. The Christian retail market was a $4.2 billion industry in 2003. During that year, it grew by more than 5 percent, which translates to about

$200 million. In 2001 music sales in general fell by 2.8 percent. This drop was the result of a general economic malaise that had hit the country in the wake of the collapse of technology stocks, illegal music downloading, and the terrorist attacks of September 11, 2001. But this economic triple whammy did not slow down Christian music sales. Christian music sales grew 13.5 percent, to 50 million units. Some estimates put the total industry at $4.5 billion in 2005.[3]

But not everyone in the evangelical world—even in the Christian publishing world—thought all was well. I quoted Christian music pioneer Michael Card earlier lamenting the fact that worship was no longer a "sacrifice," but had become a "profit center." He went on to say: "How can we talk about being 'sold out for Jesus' when TIME LIFE is selling praise and worship music in infomercials? For years the 'holy grail' was to cross over into the mainstream market, so we can have an impact on the world. But to most non-Christians, what we do may be crossing over into their pocketbooks, but not into their lives."[4]

Those involved in the industry have convinced themselves and want us to believe that this growth is a sign of God's blessing. A recent press release from the "family friendly" resort town of Branson, Missouri, says the growth of the city's tourist industry can be traced to the fact that "God, flag, and country take center stage."[5] The press release touts the fact that disgraced televangelist Jim Bakker is now producing his television program from there. It is worth noting that the press release came from a woman named Cindy Shorey, who also happens to be the daughter of country music star Mel Tillis. Mel Tillis built a 110,000-square-foot theater in Branson and later sold it to the Assemblies of God denomination for use as a conference center. Shorey now manages this conference center and promotes the town while on the denomination's payroll.

Such intertwining of personal financial interests with "ministry" activities has become common. But surely we cannot, at this point in our discussion, help but look askance at them. Indeed, one of the points of this book is that as we pursue these industrial models of ministry, industry thrives, but ministry is weakened. One of the ironies, as we are beginning to see, is that God wants the church to be the church and that even the world wants the church to be the church. It is the church that doesn't want to be the church. That's the core problem.

We have already seen how, in mostly unintentional but nonetheless very real ways, evangelicalism in the United States has departed from a Christian view of the world by rejecting a biblical view of creation and history. A close look at Christian retailing allows us to bring into focus another problem with our evangelicalism, and that is the further disintegration of community at the hands of target marketing. But in order to understand how target marketing destroys community, it may be helpful to first look at how target marketing works in one specific part of the Christian retail world: music.

The Growth of Christian Music

When contemporary Christian music emerged in the 1970s, it was enough for most Christian music consumers that the songs contained Christian lyrics. On the very few radio stations and radio programs playing Christian music, it was not unusual to hear the easy-listening pop sounds of B. J. Thomas and Amy Grant, the edgy lyrics of Larry Norman, and the heavy-metal blues/rock of the Resurrection Band being played in quick succession. Christian music began to be described as "the only genre defined by its lyrics," though no one is quite sure who originated this succinct and glib dismissal.

Those who were desperate for some alternative to the increasingly raunchy material on mainstream radio tolerated the songs they didn't like for the occasional song they did like, but this sort of formatting was almost guaranteed to fail or at least to remain on the very fringes of the radio world.

The radio world itself was undergoing a radical transformation. In the 1960s, AM ruled the radio airwaves. Atlanta was like many cities across the country. WSB-AM was the number one station in the market. It was a clear-channel, 50,000-watt station. "Clear channel" means no other station in the country could broadcast exactly on its channel or frequency of 750 AM, and it means that WSB could broadcast with the maximum power allowed by the Federal Communications Commission (FCC). Most major cities had such a "torch," as those in the industry called these powerful stations: WLS in Chicago, WWL in New Orleans, WSM in Nashville, KOMA in Oklahoma City, WCBS in New York, and KABC in Los Angeles.

WSB in Atlanta was typical. At one time the station held a 50 percent market share, which means that at any given moment, over half of the radios that were turned on were tuned to WSB. This dominance was not uncommon. All the other stations in the market split the rest of the listeners. But because there was only AM radio and because the FCC tightly regulated the number of stations in a market and the distance between the frequencies, there was plenty of audience to go around.

This situation created several phenomena. For one, this was the very tail end of the era in which radio was the most democratic and mainstream of media. A station with a 50 percent market share had children and old people, male and female, married and single in the audience. Second, the barrier against entry for new formats, such as Christian music, was enormous. There were only a limited number of stations, and those stations had to have at least 5 percent of the market to be financially viable. A format that could be expected to pull less than 1 percent of the market didn't have a chance.

So Christian music, such as it was in the early 1970s, had no radio outlet. But it did have parachurch youth organizations, independent concert promoters who were often also youth ministers, and Christian bookstores. The Christian bookstore industry was a mom-and-pop affair in those days. The Carpenter's Shop in Athens, Georgia, was typical. Dwayne Chambers was a successful local entrepreneur, church deacon, and civic leader. He owned a dry-cleaning facility that had some extra space in its building, so he started selling Christian books there. This was purely a ministry activity, a way to give back to the community for this man whose impulse to serve would eventually earn him a seat on the Athens City Council and then a long tenure as mayor.

Athens is a college town, and even before the days of R.E.M. and the B-52s, it had a vibrant music scene, so it was not unusual for kids to come into the Carpenter's Shop and ask for music. In those days Christian bookstores were often also church supply stores, carrying sheet music for choirs, and much of this music was published by Word Publishing. Word, the first exclusively gospel music label, had been started in Waco, Texas, in 1950. Its first recording artist was the classically trained baritone Frank Boggs, who ended up recording more than twenty albums of mostly hymns and gospel standards for Word and who sang at the coronation of Queen Elizabeth in 1958. By 1970 Word Records was a multi-million-dollar recording and publishing company, having bypassed secular distribution channels by going directly to retail outlets such as Chambers's Carpenter's Shop. Few people were getting rich, aside from the senior managers at Word, who ultimately became very rich; the thousands of retailers who valued the ministry component of the business were just getting by.

But things were about to drastically change in the Christian music industry. In 1969 Larry Norman had released *Upon This Rock*, which is now considered to be the first true contemporary Christian music album, though it was released on the secular label Capitol Records. And a few years later, Explo '72 brought more than eighty thousand young people to Dallas for a mass rally that became an archetype for Christian music festivals and such organizations as Promise Keepers and Women of Faith. The size of the event surprised everyone but its organizers, and it became the defining moment for what came to be called the

Jesus Movement. Billy Graham preached six different times at the event. Many young people who attended the event say their attendance at Explo was a defining moment in their lives. Greg Laurie, who later founded Harvest Crusade Ministries, was there. *The Purpose-Driven Life* author Rick Warren was there. "It was a defining moment," said Southern Evangelical Seminary president Alex McFarland, who has studied the event. "For better or for worse, Explo '72 defined what a successful ministry event looked like for many people who became leaders in the modern American church."[6] The emerging contemporary Christian music industry was represented by the top acts, including Larry Norman, Love Song, and Andre Crouch. The event made the cover of the June 30, 1972, *LIFE* magazine. Christian music—and the modern evangelical movement—was finally beginning to penetrate the popular consciousness.

Changes in technology were also contributing to the growth of the Christian-industrial complex by allowing a proliferation of radio stations with targeted Christian formats. As we will see in our discussion of the great stereopticon (in chapter six), Christian material has been on the radio from the very beginning. The very first public radio broadcast, on Christmas Eve 1906, featured a Bible reading.[7]

But in the late 1960s and early 1970s, the popularity of FM radio increased dramatically. By 1972, FM radio became standard equipment in most cars, dramatically increasing the number of viable stations. The clarity of the FM signal made it perfect for music formats. FCC limits on the number of stations a single company could own kept the prices of radio stations relatively cheap, so suddenly there was a proliferation of viable stations. Whereas in 1968, WSB-AM/Atlanta had a 50 percent market share as the number one station in the market, by 1978 WSB was barely hanging on to its number one spot, with about 20 percent of the market. Smaller stations found that they could pay the bills with as little as 2 percent of the market.

In the 1980s and 1990s technological and regulatory innovations continued, increasing the pace of change. AM stereo dramatically improved the sound quality of AM radio, breathing new life into the band and allowing further fragmentation of the medium. Digital radio began to replace analog, allowing for greater precision of both broadcasting and reception. So the FCC ruled that the distance between signals on the FM band in a given market could be decreased. In crowded metropolitan markets, that rule change created as many as five new FM stations.

Targeting Becky

With more and more stations available, the age of highly targeted programming had fully arrived. Christian music, which had quietly built an audience over the years on the backs of small, ministry-minded entrepreneurs such as Dwayne Chambers, suddenly became extremely lucrative. Amy Grant's *Age to Age* became the industry's first album to go platinum (one million in sales) in 1987. A few years later, Word Records was bought by ABC/Capital Cities in a deal that at the time was worth nearly $100 million.

The stakes became huge, and success was no longer measured the way Dwayne Chambers measured it, in changed lives. For one thing, many of the record labels were no longer owned by Christians, but by equity funds or the public markets. The new measurements for many of these companies were earnings per share and market share points. Tens of millions of dollars could be made or lost based on a single percentage point difference, more or less, in the ratings.

That's when Christian radio decided that a mythical young housewife named Becky was its target customer. If you walk into a top Christian radio station today, everyone on the staff will know Becky, though they may have a different name for her at their station, an ironic and furtive attempt to make Becky their own. Becky is the one person they want to listen. Every little thing the station does is done with Becky in mind.

"We call her Debbie," said Joe Paulo, the general manager of WRCM/Charlotte, one of the top ten Christian radio stations in the country and a finalist in the Gospel Music Association's "Station of the Year" category in 2003. "But it's the same idea."[8]

"For years, our target was the twenty-five- to forty-four-year-old female," Paulo said. "But no one is twenty-five to forty-four years old. You're either twenty-five or forty-four, and your tastes and lifestyle are very different depending on whether you're one or the other," he said.

Paulo knows exactly who Becky is and what she cares about. "She's thirty-five years old. She has two kids. She drives a minivan and is married, but her marriage is not all she dreamed it would be. She goes to church pretty regularly, but not every Sunday. She is mostly a stay-at-home mom, but she may work a few hours a week or may work seasonal jobs at different times of the year to bring a few extra dollars into the household."

Paulo also knows what Becky thinks. "She cares about issues that affect her kids," he said. "Food, education, health, family, leisure-time activities." Paulo said everything his station puts on the air must pass this test: "Will Becky care?"

That question and its answer have changed Paulo's station, as they have all of Christian radio. When WRCM went on the air in 1993, it immediately became one of the top ten radio stations in Charlotte, which is a top-twenty-five U.S. media market. But the way the station sounded in 1993 is significantly different from the way it sounds today. In 1993 the station aired news at the top of every hour. During midday and in the evening, programs from Focus on the Family and other top ministries played. Today, news is gone and so are the programs. Focus on the Family's daily thirty-minute program was dropped in part because of a show about same-sex marriage that the station judged to be too graphic for Becky and the young ears in her minivan. When Paulo asked Focus on the Family if he could air a repeat of a previous program in that show's place, Focus representatives refused, and the station chose to drop the show rather than have Focus on the Family dictate what it could or could not air.

"We love Focus on the Family and what they stand for, and we understand their point of view," Paulo said. "But we also think it is fair for us to make the final decision about what goes on our station."

This approach is working when it comes to building market share and financial strength. Paulo reports that since his station has focused on Becky, the audience for the station has increased nearly 100 percent. Salem Broadcasting, the behemoth of Christian broadcasting, has built its empire with this microtargeting approach. It now owns nearly one hundred Christian radio stations around the country and is by far the largest Christian radio broadcaster in the nation. In fact, it is number three among all station ownership groups, behind only Clear Channel and Infinity Broadcasting.

Many people who have been involved in Christian radio for many years are concerned about Salem's ascendancy. Brad Burkhart, a Christian radio consultant who helped pioneer many of the music-intensive formats that today Salem stations follow, said that many Christian radio old-timers consider Salem the antichrist of the Christian radio business. "There are lots of great radio people whose careers ended when their stations were bought by Salem," Burkhart said.

Of course, it is fair to say that—for all the reasons we've already cited—the changes that Salem brought to Christian radio would likely have been brought by market forces, if not at the hands of Salem, then by someone else. Radio station consolidation was not a Salem invention. But it is true that Salem has pursued that strategy and, through acquisition of stations and through organic growth of the stations it owns, has seen a meteoric rise. In early 2005 Salem, which is publicly traded, had a market capitalization of nearly $1 billion, though the truth is that the stock has had a roller-coaster ride of ups and downs since going public in 1999.

And though the company is on the NASDAQ stock exchange, a significant minority of the shares are still owned by the founders, Edward Atsinger and Stuart Epperson. Whatever else you can say about Salem, it has made both Atsinger and Epperson not only extraordinarily rich but also powerful in ways that money can't buy. Since 2002 Atsinger has not failed to make *TALKERS* magazine's annual list of the most powerful radio executives. He was the only Christian radio executive to make the list. Epperson has become a leading Christian activist and was named to a list of the twenty-five most influential U.S. evangelicals by *TIME* magazine. The list included Jerry Falwell, Billy Graham, and James Dobson.[9]

How Ratings Drive Liturgy and Theology

But in the realm of Christian music, the symbiosis—or parasitism—is even more pervasive because of the role contemporary Christian music has played in the so-called worship wars in the evangelical church. The worship wars are those fights that take place in churches between those who want hymns and those who want more contemporary songs. The truth is that the worship wars are much more than just a question of musical taste, but a conflict in style and preferences is often how the war presents itself.

I mention it here simply to make the point that the worship wars are perpetuated, even if unintentionally, by the marketing of contemporary Christian music. To understand this, consider that when a congregation sings Martin Luther's "A Mighty Fortress Is Our God," no money changes hands. But when that same congregation sings the popular praise and worship song "God of Wonders," written by Steve Hindalong and Marc Byrd, both men and their music publishing company get a small payday. That's because "A Mighty Fortress" is in the public domain, but "God of Wonders" belongs to them. And churches that use these songs must pay a licensing fee to an organization called Christian Copyright Licensing International (CCLI). The size of the copyright fee depends on the size of the church, but a five-hundred-member church would pay about $300 per year. Currently, approximately 140,000 churches are CCLI license holders. That means that about $50 million per year is collected and redistributed to copyright owners. And this large and growing number is just one part of a growing CCLI empire. CCLI also allows churches to pay additional fees to use movie clips as sermon illustrations.

It's probably no coincidence that the CCLI's founding in 1984 corresponds more or less with the beginning of explosive growth in the contemporary Christian music industry and with the growth of worship music in particular. CCLI provided the third leg of the stool for Christian music promoters. The growth of Christian radio provided a way to introduce new material to the market, the churches themselves started using the music in their services, and CCLI allowed the promoters to get paid by the churches that used them.

I want to be clear that CCLI is not a villain in this process. Indeed, CCLI is in some ways filling an important and vital need. Without an organization such as CCLI, the rights of songwriters to be paid for the use of their material would have no protection. Churches would be forced to break copyright laws every time they wanted to sing a contemporary song. CCLI was born of good intentions. My point, however, is one that is a theme of this book: despite these good intentions, bad consequences sometimes ensue. Good intentions are not enough. In such matters, wisdom is required.

Contrast this with the old method. Hymnbooks contain songs that are mostly in the public domain and have little or no licensing fees. They have historically been published by denominational publishers who make them available to congregations more or less at cost. They were not aggressively marketed or promoted because they are typically denominationally specific, reflecting the doctrine and liturgy of a particular church. Indeed, the selection of songs for hymnals is an elaborate, painstaking process. There is a negative side to this process. Many consider the process bureaucratic and the product staid. But one thing you can say about a denominational hymnal: it is not an accidental or incidental process, but one that has historically been considered vital to church life. This is a key point: the hymnals are informed by and reinforce the theology of the church. Said plainly, hymnals are discipleship tools.

Contemporary worship songs, on the other hand, are a revenue stream for copyright holders and music publishers.

They are aggressively promoted and now make up a significant share of the $4.5 billion Christian retail market. Indeed, no matter which side you are on in these worship wars, both sides can agree on this simple observation: for the most part, the traditionalists have lost this fight, at least in the evangelical church. Virtually every one of the one hundred largest and one hundred fastest-growing churches on *Outreach* magazine's list is a church that has one or more so-called contemporary services.

So here's the larger point: there was a time when theologians and the wisest minds of a church determined what was said and sung in a church. Today, who makes those decisions? Becky. What Becky likes gets played on Christian radio, and what gets played on Christian radio gets promoted to church musicians and church leaders, both intentionally, as a part of the machinery of the Christian-industrial complex, or unintentionally, just because these songs are on the air. The result: our churches are filled with songs not because they reflect our highest and best thinking and artistry or because they remind us and teach our children important truths, but because they are—as many Christian stations say about themselves—"safe for the entire family."

Some of us cannot hear that tagline without experiencing a bit of unintended irony. We remember C. S. Lewis's description of Aslan from *The Lion, the Witch and the Wardrobe*: "'Course he isn't safe. But he's good." The modern evangelical church, on the other hand, has become satisfied with a lion that no longer roars. The church has become safe, but no longer good.

Merry Christmas
versus Happy Holidays

I hope you will indulge me one more example before we step back and make a few general observations about the current conditions I've been laying out for you. And that example is the recent controversy over the usage of the greeting *Merry Christmas* instead of the greeting *Happy Holidays*. I want to explore this controversy briefly, not so much because it is the most important battle in the culture war, but because it provides examples of the pathologies we have discussed—the triumph of sentimentality and the new provincialism—as well as shows how the gears of the Christian-industrial complex work.

In a nutshell, beginning in the 1990s, but most especially in the early years of the twenty-first century, some conservative Christian groups decided that the use of the phrase *Happy Holidays* instead of *Merry Christmas* is a defeat of Christian values by the forces of political correctness. These groups include, but are not limited to, the Mississippi-based American Family Association (AFA) and the Alliance Defense Fund (ADF), a legal aid group that was formed as a cooperative venture by a number of Christian groups as a Christian counterweight to the American Civil Liberties Union. Among the founders and financial supporters of the ADF are Focus on the Family and the Family Research Council.

Before looking at the current controversy, it is important to note that the celebration of Christmas has always been a source of tension among Christians. The early church did not celebrate Christmas. In fact, several early church fathers specifically condemned the celebration of the birth of Jesus. The earliest references to it appear in the fourth century.[10] However, the focus of these early holy days—or holidays, as they came to be called—was on Epiphany, which occurred a couple of weeks after the solstice (in part to avoid confusion with the pagan celebrations). And Epiphany celebrated not the birth of Jesus, but his baptism.

The celebration of Christmas as we know it today with trees, tinsel, gift giving, and all the rest is a nineteenth-century phenomenon, and the modern Christmas traditions were done more to diminish than to accentuate the Christian elements.

When Christianity came to northern Europe, where winter nights were long, the winter solstice celebrations were firmly entrenched. From the eleventh to the nineteenth centuries, Christmas was not much celebrated by devout Christians, in part because it had more of the characteristics of a bacchanal than a contemplative Christian holy day. In the seventeenth century the Puritans attempted to eliminate the observance of Christmas altogether, believing it an unholy combination of the pagan and the "popish" and because it resulted in much public drunkenness. For these reasons, in some New England towns the observance of Christmas was actually prohibited by law.

In fact, it is ironic that many of the defenders of Christmas, who often also venerate our founding fathers, forget that one of the deciding battles of the Revolutionary War took place when George Washington forced his troops across the Delaware River on Christmas night 1776. He attacked Hessian troops at Trenton, routing them in a battle that lasted only an hour. The myth spread that the Hessian troops were unprepared for the battle because they were drunk or hung over from their drunken celebration of Christmas. It's likely that this story is not strictly true, but it caught on because of the American and Puritan disdain for the celebration of Christmas.[11]

Most historians attribute the rise in popularity of Christmas to Charles Dickens, who was no advocate of biblical Christianity. The celebration of Christmas was almost nonexistent in this country when Dickens—already the best-known writer in the world—published *A Christmas Carol*, one of his most popular stories, in 1843. But Dickens wrote the story more out of an impulse toward social reform than out of any desire to promote Christianity.

This forgotten history of Christmas makes the current defense of it by evangelical groups seem almost ridiculous. In other words, to defend the modernist celebrations of a "Merry Christmas" as superior to the more ancient notions of "Happy Holy Days" reflects a real historical illiteracy. The absurdity is compounded when you consider what a materialistic debauchery the holiday has become. It's hard to imagine humble Mary and Joseph being at all comfortable with what Christmas has become, let alone the carpenter from Nazareth himself, whose only recorded fit of anger was displayed by the overturning of the money changers' tables in the temple. In fact, you could make a case that the Christian response to the December 25 holiday would be to keep Jesus as far away from it as possible.

So what possible purpose could be served by "keeping Christ in Christmas" when Christmas is what it is? The answer to that appeared in a story published by Religion News Service (RNS) the week before Christmas 2006. "The Mississippi-based American Family Association says it has sold more than 500,000 buttons and 125,000 bumper stickers bearing the slogan 'Merry Christmas: It's Worth Saying,'" the RNS story began.[12]

The story then said the Alliance Defense Fund had sold "about 20,000 'Christmas packs.' The packs, available for a suggested $29 donation, included a three-page legal memo and two lapel pins." In other words, the "Christmas Wars" netted the ADF about one-half million dollars. This money was a true windfall to an organization that, according to MinistryWatch. com, had a 2004 budget of about $19 million and listed nearly $20 million in cash on its balance sheet.

The story goes beyond the ridiculous to the surreal when you learn that the groups also publish a "naughty and nice" list that identifies major retailers that use the words *Merry Christmas* in their Christmas advertising as "nice" and those that use *Happy Holidays* as "naughty"—as if identifying Jesus with the worst aspects of the season's materialism is something to be celebrated.

Tim Wildmon, president of the AFA, told RNS, "It's a way to fight back against the secular progressives and promote the real meaning of Christmas."

But it's no surprise that it also made these groups an easy target for its enemies. "It's just a fund-raising scam," said the Reverend Barry Lynn, executive director of Americans United for the Separation of Church and State, in the same RNS story. "And it's a scam in the worst sense—it's fighting something that doesn't even exist."

Nonetheless, the AFA's sale of 500,000 buttons and 100,000 magnets was so successful that Wildmon told RNS that the group planned to make Easter buttons beginning in 2007.

Vocation and Community

But not everyone is excited about the industrialization of the Christian market. Michael Card was a part of the first wave of Christian music in the early 1970s, playing in churches and coffeehouses and releasing critically acclaimed and financially viable, if not best-selling, albums. His greatest successes came as a songwriter—his "El Shaddai" has been recorded by dozens of artists and was a million seller for Amy Grant—and as a singer of lullabies. Card's *Sleep Sound in Jesus* was certified gold (500,000 units sold) by the Recording Industry Association of America in 1994, and it continues to be a steady seller.

So Card's criticism of the industry can't be dismissed as the sour grapes of an outsider. For more than twenty years he has been an industry insider. But he said there's plenty of blame to go around.[13]

"I trace a lot of what is wrong with contemporary Christian music to the fact that in the early days the church closed the door on us," Card said. "And in the late '80s, when the church invited us back, they invited us back for the wrong reasons. It was about power and money. Christian music became popular and profitable, and the church wanted a piece of this. Those are the wrong reasons, but churches too have become industrial."

For Card, the dividing line in this debate is this very conflict between community and industry. And he said it is not a question merely of style or taste, but of theology. "When we first meet God," Card said, "he is an artist. He's a painter, basically, stepping back and forth from a canvas. It is a shame the church has overlooked this, because the tools you need to be an artist are the same tools you need to be a disciple. You need a servant's heart, you need obedience to a call from God, and you need humility, teachability."

That discipleship and artisanship are closely related activities is a critical point. The megachurch and the Christian-industrial complex have an inkling that something is missing and at a certain point will tack on "arts ministry" to their cafeteria menu of offerings. But arts ministries miss the point. Such ministries often have the feel of being mere brand extensions of the church and not an attempt to integrate beauty and truth into public and communal worship. In other words, if the church has grown to the point that it has a youth ministry and a young adult ministry and a small-group ministry and all the other normal ministries, then to continue to grow or to reach an untapped market it probably needs an arts ministry. What the church should do instead is to disciple all its members, and this spiritual formation necessarily includes helping the members discern and develop their gifts. Because we are created in the image of the Creator, our artistic gifts will emerge from all of us, not just the "artsy" among us.[14]

So while having an arts ministry under these circumstances may (or may not) be better than nothing, it does not seem to be what Card is getting at. Nurturing artists and art is not separate from or other than the process of disciple making; they are all the same thing if disciple making is truly the process of helping us be more like God.

It is therefore no coincidence that the explosive growth of the Christian market, the proliferation in the number of mega-churches, and the general spiritual malaise of the church and the culture have all occurred simultaneously. One pathology feeds the other. Or, more accurately and metaphorically, they are the three sides of the same coin. One side of the coin is the megachurch, one side is the growth of the Christian market, and the small third side of the coin—the edge that we don't notice and don't talk about—is the spiritual malaise. But it is that edge of the coin that turns the screw, the turning of which adds to the anxiety and fear that church and true art are supposed to relieve.

If Card's diagnosis is accurate, what is his prescription? Michael Card offered this: "The question I would ask the indus-trial church and the industrial entertainment world is this: What is your basis? The basis of any industry is money and power. The basis of community is letting go of money and power. Unqualified acceptance is not based on performance. Unqualified acceptance is the hallmark of community, which is what the church should be." Card said that "at the point it becomes about money and power and more people and a bigger building—despite the best of intentions—the more delicate aspects of community become trampled."

Aiming for Authenticity

Michael Card has chosen to remain more or less in the world of contemporary Christian music, hoping to reform it from within. But a growing number of Christian artists or "artists who are Christians," as Card prefers to be called, have quietly stepped outside of the CCM world to play secular venues, self-produce records, and sometimes struggle financially so they can create music they consider to be more authentic.

Buddy and Julie Miller have been called the first couple of Americana. Buddy Miller is Emmylou Harris's band leader, and he has a long list of credits as a guitar player and producer on Christian records. Julie Miller even recorded a couple of albums on Christian labels before moving to a secular label.

But around 2001, with the release of the movie *O Brother, Where Art Thou?*, roots music or Americana music or alt-country music crossed over into the mainstream. Buddy and Julie Miller, now well into middle age, were finally hitting it big, or bigger than they had ever hit it before in their twenty-five-year career. Few Americana acts play the big arenas, but the Millers suddenly found they could make small and midsized venues look full, and their albums were selling steadily.

Typical of their latest tour was a near-sold-out show at Charlotte's Neighborhood Theatre, a seven-hundred-seat venue that had recently hosted Wilco and the Nitty Gritty Dirt Band. After the show and well after midnight, I interviewed Julie Miller about her involvement in the Christian music scene and her current career as one of the queens of Americana. She had nothing against Christian music, but said, "I just don't see myself in those terms."

"Christian music is the only musical form that is defined by its lyrics," she said, using a line heard often in conversations with

Christian musicians who are uncomfortable with the label. She thinks some Christian artists want to go the CCM route because it's "easy and safe."

"When Jesus healed the man possessed by demons, he asked Jesus what we all would ask," Miller said. "He said, 'Jesus, can I go with you?' Amazingly, Jesus said no. He told the man to stay and let others see how he had been healed. Going with Jesus would have been easy and safe, but Jesus himself told the man to stay behind." Miller said that was her experience. "I had this incredible Damascus road experience," she said. "Jesus interrupted my life." But she said that was no reason to retreat into the world of contemporary Christian music. "I don't want to do music that is contrived," she said. "I'd rather hear an old woman sing 'Amazing Grace' *a capella* than some of the overproduced stuff I hear today."

Bill Mallonee agrees. A product of the same robust and diverse Athens, Georgia, music scene that brought the world R.E.M. and the B-52s, Mallonee doesn't look like a Protestant church elder—but he is, or at least he was. Though steeped in Reformed and evangelical theology, with a particular fondness for Francis Schaeffer and others who talk about how art can impact the culture, Mallonee left evangelicalism (and, it must be said, a failed marriage) behind and is now a practicing Roman Catholic. He may be the most famous Christian musician you've never heard of. For years he fronted the band Vigilantes of Love. VOL was a crowd favorite, achieving near-legendary status at Cornerstone, the "granddaddy" of the Christian outdoor summer music and arts festivals. VOL kicked around on several marginal

Christian music labels before Mallonee figured out he could do the kinds of albums he wanted by producing them himself with some of the same talented Athens music-scene players—such as John Keene and R.E.M.'s Peter Buck—who had worked with Widespread Panic, Wilco, and the B-52s.

These self-produced and Keene- and Buck-produced albums were listened to by the cognoscenti of the secular and Christian music worlds. The band seemed to be about to break through to mainstream acceptance when it signed a deal with the storied label Capricorn. After one critically acclaimed album with Capricorn, an album that the label didn't have the resources to effectively market, Capricorn imploded. Now, Mallonee performs solo, banging around the country in a van with a license plate that says "Struggleville," and his act includes a reminder to his audience to remember the bartender with a generous tip before you leave.[15]

Mallonee is fond of describing his music with the old line of the traveling troubadour: "four chords and the truth." Of course, only those in the know remember that the original line, from Woody Guthrie, is "three chords and the truth." It's Mallonee's understated way of saying that he brings something extra to the party. Even his fans don't always get it, but that understatement and that irony are the secrets of Mallonee's genius and why he labors in relative obscurity. But what his fans know is that there are about a dozen ways to play every chord and that for every major chord there is also a minor chord.

And, it seems, until Christians discover *that* truth, the audiences of artists like Bill Mallonee and Buddy and Julie Miller may end up being not unlike how the poet John Milton described his readers: "fit, though few."[16]

God and Mammon

Two of the best known verses in Scripture relate to money: "The love of money is a root of all kinds of evil," and "No one can serve two masters. Either he will hate the one and love the other, or he will be devoted to the one and despise the other. You cannot serve both God and Money" (1 Timothy 6:10; Matthew 6:24).

Those involved in the Christian-industrial complex—people like Branson's Cindy Shorey—naturally defend their motives. When I first wrote about Branson in an editorial for the Evangelical Press News Service called "Deliver Us from Branson," I received more feedback than usual, both scathing denunciations from Shorey and others who make a living in Branson as well as friendly invitations from some resort owners to visit—at their expense—to see the place for myself.

These are common reactions from those in the Christian-industrial complex, whether they be show promoters in Branson or Merry Christmas promoters in Tupelo: if you can't be bought off, you are denounced as anti-Christian.

It is this inability to accept criticism or to be self-critical that distinguishes the Christian-industrial complex and is its greatest danger. The church operating in *koinonia*, true community, is the antidote to this poisonous industrial model. The two most vital, distinguishing characteristics of those who live in *koinonia* are humility and accountability. These are precisely the two characteristics that the Christian-industrial complex cannot tolerate.

In short, the rise of the Christian-industrial complex is the great destroyer of *koinonia*. And nowhere has this industrial model been more evident in the evangelical church than in the area of what I have come to call body-count evangelism—which is where we turn our attention next.

CHAPTER 5

BODY-COUNT EVANGELISM

The paradox is that a genuine "love for souls" [is] diverted by fashionable modes into a mere "winning" of them [and] a total misuse of people for alleged evangelical "results." The consequence is a loss of respect for people and their souls, and the withering of the original concern and love.

—G. W. TARGET IN *EVANGELISM INC.* (1968)

The idea at the heart of the modern evangelical movement is this: Sharing the good news of Jesus Christ is a primary responsibility of Christians, and seeing the lost come to know Christ is the first and most urgent responsibility of our time.

Because the end is near and Christ is coming soon, it's vital that we share the gospel with as many people as quickly as possible. "The one thing you can't do in heaven," wrote evangelical leader Mark Cahill, "is tell others about Jesus."[1]

Because of that reality, many evangelicals insist, any modern means may be employed: modern management techniques, sophisticated direct mail, mass evangelistic rallies, radio, and television. So the modern megachurch and parachurch ministries, especially the largest ones, have made huge investments in these capabilities. According to their own tax returns, Billy Graham Evangelistic Association in 2005 took in more than $100 million in donations. Focus on the Family's revenue exceeded $150 million. The Trinity Broadcasting Network (TBN) received more than $180 million. Most of their expenses are related to media, either the production of programming or the buying of time on stations so that their programming can be seen and heard.

And all of the organizations mentioned, and many others besides, have a wealth that would have seemed unimaginable to Christian ministries in the pre-electronic age. Indeed, TBN has had more than one-half billion dollars in operating surpluses over the past decade. The organization's balance sheet shows more than $250 million in cash and liquid assets on hand, and yet they continue to spend a significant amount of programming time asking for money.[2]

In fact, according to MinistryWatch.com, the ten largest Christian ministries in the United States had a combined revenue in 2004 in excess of $4.6 billion. By contrast, consider that the average Protestant church in this country attracts only about ninety adults on a typical weekend, according to pollster George Barna. The average budget of these average churches is less than $200,000 a year.[3]

In other words, the money being donated to only the ten largest Christian ministries would fully support more than twenty thousand average churches. The question suggested by these data is this: What is the highest and best use of these funds? To support ten huge ministries or to support twenty thousand local churches?

The answer to that question is not so simple, and in at least one sense the question is not fair. Neither God's economy nor the human economy is a zero-sum game. It's possible that these megaministries may not be robbing the local church. Possible, but given what we have seen so far, unlikely. Nonetheless, for now, we will leave that an open question.

But given that the megachurch and the parachurch grew dramatically in the last half of the twentieth century, it is fair, at least, to ask those questions as well as these: Are the church of Jesus Christ and the culture in which it operates in better shape or worse shape than fifty years ago? And whatever the difference—for better or worse—was the growth of the megachurch and the parachurch the cause of the change or just coincident with the change?

These are the open questions we will attempt to answer. But whatever investment you may have in the answer to these questions, almost no one would disagree with my presupposition that these ministries have become a dominant feature of the evangelical landscape since World War II.

The Rise of the Parachurch Organization

Large organizations such as Focus on the Family and mass evangelistic rallies such as the kind made popular by Billy

Graham are so much a part of evangelicalism today that it is hard to remember there was a time not so long ago when such organizations did not dominate the evangelical landscape.

The Greek prefix *para* means "alongside." So the word *para-church* means "alongside the church," and that definition itself goes a long way toward explaining why parachurch organizations did not exist until recently: the church generally did not need ancillary organizations to come "alongside" of it. That's not to say that associations did not exist. As we saw in chapter one, Americans have long been prone to form associations. Alexis de Tocqueville noted this tendency in us during his famous tour in the mid-nineteenth century. Indeed, he said it was part of the genius of the American experiment in democracy. Robert Bellah and the coauthors of *Habits of the Heart*, a classic analysis of American cultural norms, wrote that "America is a nation of joiners." Bellah noted that Americans are much more likely to join a voluntary association than are the citizens of any other nation in the world.[4]

But it is important to note that these associations were most often secular societies. They frequently had a benevolent purpose, but they were also usually nonreligious in nature. Indeed, associations were often promoted by those who wanted to diminish, not increase, the role of religion in the public square. Benjamin Franklin, for example, was a great promoter of associations. But his promotion of associations of all types—from Philadelphia's (and the nation's) first volunteer fire department to the American Philosophical Society, America's oldest learned society—grew as his disdain for organized religion also grew.[5]

But if Franklin's impulses were antireligious, they were almost as strongly antigovernmental, at least so far as it related to social welfare. Franklin noted that the government-run welfare system of Great Britain encouraged laziness. His view was shared by many in the colonies, secular and religious alike. So, private societies formed to meet the needs of the poor and otherwise unfortunate, including widows and orphans. Marvin Olasky's *The Tragedy of American Compassion* notes that many of these organizations—unlike those in the line founded by Franklin—did have a strongly religious character, in part because of scriptural mandates to care for the poor. Olasky documented this movement, which, by the 1830s, had "tens of thousands of points of light" dedicated to everything from the establishment of public sanitation schemes to the establishment of orphanages.[6]

It's important to note, however, that these organizations did not much resemble parachurch groups of today. For one thing, the United States had no income tax until 1913, when the Sixteenth Amendment to the Constitution was ratified. Of course, with no income tax, there was no financial incentive to donate money to benevolent associations. The organizations existed solely for the purposes for which they were created. If they were effective, the funding continued from private sources. But if they were not effective or the need was met, the funding generally evaporated.

With the additional incentive of a tax deduction, the implicit contract between organizations and donors subtly changed. Organizations and their donors could provide benefits to each other without necessarily providing benefits to the community or to individuals the organizations were ostensibly created to serve. That partly explains why the number of tax-exempt organizations in the United States has grown steadily throughout the twentieth century. In 1998 there were more than 730,000 religious tax-exempt organizations. (This number includes churches.) That number had increased by nearly 200,000 in the decade of the '90s alone. The *CPA Journal* estimated that tax-exempt organizations—the majority of them religious in nature—take in more than $600 billion per year and employ 7 percent of the U.S. work force.[7] It is easy to see how the rise of the parachurch has contributed to the growth of the Christian-industrial complex.

By contrast, as the parachurch arose, the church went into decline. The Leadership Network estimated there are only about 300,000 Protestant churches in the United States.[8] I say *only* because while 300,000 is a large number, you can see that the number of parachurch organizations is now significantly larger than the number of churches. And even though the population of the United States has doubled since 1950 and the number of parachurch organizations has increased by a geometric factor during that time, the number of churches (as we said in chapter one) has either remained steady or declined.

These data do not conclusively prove that the rise of parachurch organizations has actually damaged the vitality of the church, but that possibility cannot be ignored. That there is no relationship whatsoever strains credulity.

Before the Parachurch

In chapter two, when I introduced the idea of the new provincialism (to recap: our dismissal of the lessons of history), I also introduced to our discussion the Great Awakening of the eighteenth century and the so-called Second Great Awakening of the nineteenth century. I did so because in introducing the idea of the new provincialism, it is important to realize that in many ways the Second Great Awakening *was* an intentional rejection of the past. I also did so because it is important for us to see that modern evangelicalism has much more in common with the Second Great Awakening than the first, though we, for the most part, have forgotten that.

The Second Great Awakening also has much to teach us about the rise of the parachurch and the phenomenon of body-count evangelism that has come to typify modern evangelicalism.

Indeed, one of the most significant differences between the two awakenings is the fact that during the First Great Awakening, mass rallies were virtually nonexistent, but in the Second Great Awakening they were common. To be sure, there were practical reasons that prevented mass rallies in the early 1700s. Most obvious is that many cities of the day had just a few hundred to a few thousand inhabitants. In 1700 the Anglo population of the American colonies was less than 300,000 inhabitants. Boston, perhaps the largest city in America at that time, had about 7,000 inhabitants.

Jonathan Edwards was born into this world of small towns—towns always on the edge of the frontier—in 1703. The son and grandson of ministers, he entered Yale at age thirteen and was preaching the gospel by age twenty. He pastored the Congregational Church in Northampton, Massachusetts, from 1729 to 1750, but he preached in other churches in the region. By 1733 the revival we now call the Great Awakening broke out in Northampton. Over the course of about six months, around three hundred people were added to the rolls of the churches in which he preached. The First Great Awakening resulted in the conversion of thousands, if not tens of thousands, of people, and—as we said earlier—historians say it played a role in both the ability and the willingness of the colonists to bear the privations that came as a result of the American Revolution.[9]

But, as I have suggested, the modern evangelical movement has much more in common with the Second Great Awakening than with the first. The differences between these two were not superficial, but they are almost forgotten today. We often speak of the First Great Awakening and the Second Great Awakening almost as a single phenomenon. But, of course, if this book is about anything, it is about these concepts: theology matters, history matters, and ideas have consequences.

So, to truly understand what is happening today, let's take a look at a couple of the most significant theological and historical differences between then and now.

The Sovereignty of God

Most biographies of Edwards say that he was a great apologist for Reformation theology, and Calvinism in particular. And there is enough truth in that to let it stand for now. But it would be more generally accurate to say that Edwards had a strong sense of, and preached, the sovereignty of God. Jonathan Edwards believed—and in this he shared common cause with other Reformers—that God is in complete control of his universe and that it defies logic and is an affront to God to believe that humans can do anything that hastens or speeds salvation.

In short, God and God alone redeems souls. Even our ability to choose, including our desire to choose God, comes from God himself.

So it is no surprise that the early sermons of Edwards's career—including those in Boston and Northampton in the early 1730s that led to the first revival outbreaks of the Great Awakening—were not what we would today call evangelistic sermons, but were disputations against Arminianism.

Arminianism is a brand of Protestant thought founded by the Dutch theologian Jacobus Arminius. By the time Arminius started writing and teaching in the late 1500s, Calvin had been dead for a generation; but Calvin's ideas were already dominant in the Protestant churches of both Europe and America. The intellectual rigor and the firm scriptural basis of Calvin's *Institutes*, which defined his theological ideas, caused them to be quickly adopted by Protestants of many stripes.

But Arminius found them dry and stale. He said they were "deterministic." If Calvin was right, and that even the ability to choose God was born of God, did that not mean that the ability to reject God must be born of God, too? If evil is rebellion against God, and hell a state of eternal separation from God, did that therefore not make God the author of evil and hell?

Arminius argued that people have a free will given them by God. He acknowledged that some are "elect." Scripture asserts it and common sense and plain observation make that truth undeniable. But Arminius argued that what Scripture refers to is an "election of believers." Theologians have come to call that "conditional election." If you believe, then you are part of the elect.

Calvinists responded that this idea violates both logic and orthodoxy. If God's grace can be resisted, then God is not omnipotent. Calvin and his followers argued that God is sovereign and that all other doctrines must conform to that central truth.

It is clear that Jonathan Edwards and the theology of the Great Awakening were Calvinistic. It is also clear that modern evangelicalism is Arminian. Both sides generally acknowledge as much.[10]

But which is true? Before we make an attempt to answer that question, let's look at another key aspect of Great Awakening theology and contrast it to the theology of modern evangelicalism.

Human Sinfulness

The First Great Awakening also preached human sinfulness. Indeed, we need go no further than the title of Jonathan Edwards's most famous sermon, a defining document of the Great Awakening, to see that the sinfulness of humans is a central idea. That sermon is "Sinners in the Hands of an Angry God." In it Edwards stated, "O sinner! Consider the fearful danger you are in: it is a great furnace of wrath, a wide and bottomless pit, full of the fire of wrath, that you are held over in the hand of that

God, whose wrath is provoked and incensed as much against you, as against many of the damned in hell."

To Edwards and to Reformation preachers and theologians in general, the idea that people are sinful and—apart from the grace of God—will receive God's wrath was a given.

Much of modern evangelicalism ignores this doctrine, which theologians sometimes call the human depravity or original sin.[11] We have already seen, in chapter two, how megachurch preachers such as Joel Osteen downplay our sinfulness and God's wrath and judgment. The doctrine of original sin is so often ignored that psychiatrist Karl Menninger wrote a book on the subject over thirty years ago: *Whatever Became of Sin?*[12]

The theology of the First Great Awakening includes, of course, much more than these two doctrines: the sovereignty of God and human depravity. But I mention these two doctrines here for a couple of reasons. First, they are essential, not accidental doctrines. Our beliefs about the sovereignty of God, in fact, define our worship. We worship either the omnipotent God of Scripture, or we worship some other god.

Likewise, our view of human depravity determines our Christology, our view of who Christ is. If we are not sinful, then Christ died in vain, because we need no Savior. If you argue that Jesus came not to save, but to teach, then you have to deal with his own claims to be "the way and the truth and the life. No one comes to the Father except through me" (John 14:6). If Jesus is not the Savior, then this claim is outrageous. As C. S. Lewis famously said, it is the claim of a lunatic, not a great teacher.

A Cultural Divide

The First Great Awakening was largely a church-based and urban phenomenon. Jonathan Edwards was one of the best-educated persons in the country, ordained in a mainline church, and preached mostly in the pulpits of established congregations. The Second Great Awakening, on the other hand, was mostly a rural and parachurch phenomenon.[13]

On the frontier, established churches were few and separated by great distances. Ordained clergy were even more scarce than pulpits. In this milieu the camp meeting began. The word would go out that on certain dates, at certain locations, religious meetings would take place. Because of the distances involved, many families would come prepared to camp, often for days and sometimes for weeks. The meetings therefore became social as well as religious events. Indeed, many would come who had no religious inclinations, but were curious or looking for a break from the rigors and isolation of frontier life.

And the preachers at these events, recognizing an opportunity to share the gospel with these nonbelievers, often turned the camp meetings into evangelistic events. As we said in chapter two, one such series of meetings took place at Cane Ridge, Kentucky, in August 1801. Most historians place the number in attendance at more than ten thousand. Some say as many as twenty thousand could have come and gone at different times during the event. Often, a half-dozen preachers would be preaching at one time, some on open-air stages built for the event and some protected from the sun by arbors made of brush, which caused some to call the events "brush arbor revivals." Often, though, preachers would merely find a spot more or less out of earshot of the stages and other preachers and stand on stumps.

The Cane Ridge Revival is often identified as the beginning of the Second Great Awakening. Many who were there went back to their own communities and organized similar events. It is believed that many thousands of people made professions of faith in Christ, and many of them became involved in established churches. Methodists, in particular, saw their numbers increase during this time. It is also true that many new churches and denominations were formed, particularly so-called holiness churches.

From Cane Ridge, revivals spread east and north. In 1802 and 1803 the revival came to the Carolinas, and by the 1820s camp meetings were being held all across the country.

What caused this revival? Of course, many ascribe it to the work of the Holy Spirit. And there can be no doubt that, by God's grace, many genuine conversions took place during this period. But it is also true that the times were pregnant with possibilities—economical, cultural, and social. On the very days the Cane Ridge Revival was breaking out, President Thomas Jefferson was negotiating with the French for possession of New Orleans, negotiations that ultimately led to the Louisiana Purchase and westward expansion. The revivalism of the Second Great Awakening is inextricably linked with the adolescent hubris of an expanding nation. This may be what theologian Stanley Hauerwas meant when he said that by the late twentieth century the problem with the American church was its being "more American than it is church."[14]

But few people were offering such an analysis during the period of the Second Great Awakening, certainly not the man who came to be one of its towering figures and a personality who helped define modern evangelicalism: Charles Finney.

Finney Men

Billy Graham and Jerry Falwell have called Charles Finney a hero. Theologian Michael Horton has not been so complimentary.[15] But both his admirers and his detractors agree that Finney was, perhaps, the defining religious figure of the nineteenth century.

The basic facts of Finney's life make it clear that he was not only a central figure of the Second Great Awakening but he was also in many ways the very embodiment of it. Born in 1792, Finney was still a child when the Cane Ridge Revival broke out. And while the Second Great Awakening began as a southern phenomenon, Finney was a Yankee clear through: born in Connecticut, converted to Christianity at age twenty-nine while a lawyer in New York, and an abolitionist his entire life. Finney was an architect of revivalist preaching, but he was also a product of it.

Finney gave up his law practice almost immediately after his conversion in order to begin preaching. He had no college degree, and though he ultimately wrote a systematic theology, he was basically a self-taught theologian. He was originally ordained a Presbyterian, and during his ordination examination he was asked if he subscribed to the Calvinistic doctrines of the Westminster Confession. His reply, which he later recounted in his memoir, has been a primary text for his critics who cite it as evidence of Finney's willingness to play fast and loose with the truth: "Unexpectedly to myself they asked me if I received the Confession of faith of the Presbyterian church. I had not examined it;—that is, the large work, containing the Catechisms and Presbyterian Confession. This had made no part of my study. I replied that I received it for substance of doctrine, so far as I understood it. But I spoke in a way that plainly implied, I think, that I did not pretend to know much about it." [16]

Finney explicitly rejected the doctrine of the sovereignty of God, a bulwark of the First Great Awakening, when he wrote, "A revival of religion is not a miracle, nor dependent on a miracle in any sense. It is a purely philosophical result of the right use of the constituted means—as much so as any other effect produced by the application of means." [17] With this statement, Finney not only rejected salvation by grace but also opened the door to the use of emotionalism and technique to produce a high body count when it came time to sing the hymn of invitation at the close of the service.

Likewise, he rejected the doctrine of original sin. "A nature sinful in itself, a total inability to accept Christ and to obey God, condemnation to eternal death for the sin of Adam and for a sinful nature," Finney wrote in his memoirs, "and all the kindred and resultant dogmas of that peculiar school [Calvinism], have been the stumbling block of believers and the ruin of sinners." [18]

So Finney rejected the two core doctrines of the First Great Awakening. Little wonder theologian R. C. Sproul called Finney a heretic. That Jerry Falwell and Billy Graham admire him says a great deal about what is wrong—at least theologically speaking—with modern evangelicalism.

Finney's belief that the end justifies the means began the trend of body-count evangelism. Jonathan Edwards believed his responsibility was obedience, which meant to proclaim the gospel with integrity. The results were not his responsibility. Finney, who began his career as a lawyer and went on to be a college president, measured results. His followers began a trend toward counting the number of salvations a particular event produced. Finney's biographer, Keith J. Hardman, stated that Finney was responsible for the salvation of "hundreds of thousands."[19] Many sources cite the number of a half million—a nice, round number that, while possibly close to the number of people who made some sort of a profession of faith, can't possibly be accurate.

Sproul is one of a growing number who disdain this sort of body-count evangelism. Sproul faults Finney not only on the doctrinal points we have discussed (the sovereignty of God and the reality of original sin) but on other vital points as well. Sproul says Finney "categorically rejected substitutionary atonement and justification by faith alone."[20]

And Sproul stated plainly the problems with body-count evangelism when he said, "Everyone who has faith is called to profess faith, but not everybody who professes faith has faith. We are not saved by a profession of faith. A lot of people, it seems to me, in the evangelical world, believe that if they have walked the walk, raised the hand, signed the card—that is, made some kind of methodological profession of faith—that they're saved."[21]

This statement is an affront to much of modern evangelicalism, but it should be familiar to anyone who knows the teachings of Jesus: "Not everyone who says to me, 'Lord, Lord,' will enter the kingdom of heaven, but only he who does the will of my Father who is in heaven" (Matthew 7:21).

Lions in Winter

As I have said before, ideas have consequences. And ideas bear consequences, to borrow a biblical phrase, "after their own kind." In other words, good ideas have positive consequences, and bad ideas have negative effects. That's why a sense of history is so important, because consequences don't often show up immediately. Without a sense of history—in other words, when we embrace what I am calling the new provincialism—we tend to associate current events (incorrectly) with current or proximate causes, failing to see how bad ideas play themselves out over time.

So what were the consequences of Finney's ideas? That question has at least two answers. First, there are the consequences of Finney's own work, and second, there is the spiritual, cultural, and intellectual legacy he left behind.

On the first count, Finney himself came to believe his revival meetings had little, if any, lasting impact: "I was often instrumental in bringing Christians under great conviction, and into a state of temporary repentance and faith . . . . [But] falling short of urging them up to a point, where they would become so acquainted with Christ as to abide in Him, they would of course soon relapse into their former state."[22] Indeed, the site of some of Finney's best-known revivals, western New York, came to be known as the "burnt-over district." The revivalist fires ignited by Finney, after they cooled, left scars, but neither heat nor light. One of the most poignant assessments comes from one of Finney's own associates, Asa Mahan, quoted by B. B. Warfield—who wrote several scathing accounts of Finney's ministry. Warfield wrote,

> [Everyone] who was concerned in these revivals suffered a sad subsequent lapse: the people were left like a dead coal which could not be reignited; the pastors were shorn of all their spiritual power; and the evangelists— "among them all," [Mahan] says, "and I was personally acquainted with nearly every one of them—I cannot recall a single man, brother Finney and father Nash excepted, who did not after a few years lose his unction, and become equally disqualified for the office of evangelist and that of pastor."
>
> Thus the great "Western Revivals" ran out into disaster. . . . Over and over again, when he proposed to revisit one of the churches, delegations were sent him or other means used, to prevent what was thought of as an affliction. . . . Even after a generation had passed by, these burnt children had no liking for the fire.[23]

Finney's own theology devolved into greater and greater heresy. He denied the substitutionary atonement of Christ and other core Christian doctrines. And because many of the "converts" at Finney's and other Second Great Awakening meetings were left to fend for themselves theologically, many churches and denominations that were formed in the wake of the Second Great Awakening either quickly folded or likewise devolved into heresy.

The denomination that most plainly traces its roots to the Cane Ridge Revival, the Cumberland Presbyterians, grew rapidly through the nineteenth century. It was one of the largest denominations in the country by the 1880s. But it also became the first Reformed denomination to ordain women, and it re-wrote the Westminster Confession to eliminate "objectionable language."[24] From the 1890s until around 1910, the size of the denomination shrank by at least two-thirds. The denomination still exists; its primary presence is a few dozen congregations in Kentucky and Tennessee.

Perhaps most tellingly, some of the significant cults of the twentieth century trace their histories to the revivalism of the Second Great Awakening.[25] William Miller was a Baptist preacher and significant figure of the Second Great Awakening. His strongly premillennial theology caused him to set various dates for the return of Christ. These "Millerites" became disillusioned when the dates—in 1843 and 1844—came and went. Many of them stopped following Miller, but did not give up on spirituality. Millerites played key roles in the founding of the Jehovah's Witness and the Bahá'i faiths.

Mormonism was indirectly a fruit of the Second Great Awakening. Mormon founder Joseph Smith, born in 1805 in Vermont, moved to Palmyra in western New York. Palmyra became the site of intense revivalism. Indeed, it became part of the "burnt-over district" that became hardened to biblical

Christianity. It would be unfair and historically inaccurate to blame Finney for Mormonism. Though Finney was a dozen years older than Joseph Smith and began preaching around the state of New York when Smith was still a teen, it is unlikely that their paths ever crossed. It is more accurate to say that they both sprang from the same revivalist fire that ultimately consumed the state. What is not in dispute is that today Mormonism claims thirteen million adherents and is one of the fastest-growing religious groups in the world.

With this bitter spiritual legacy, it is somewhat surprising that Finney and the Second Great Awakening have both been so uncritically embraced by much of modern evangelicalism. But they have. And that leads us to one more question: Will modern evangelicalism reform itself or devolve further into the apostasy that ultimately enveloped Finney?

To answer that question, it might be instructive to take a look at the latter years of the ministry of the man who has all but defined modern evangelicalism: Billy Graham.

As Billy Graham reached the end of his long life, he retreated for increasingly extended periods of time to his home in the western North Carolina town of Montreat. In 1995 he did a homecoming crusade in his hometown of Charlotte, North Carolina. He was old, he said, and this could be his final crusade. But that "final" crusade in Charlotte ended up being followed by many more, including a 2006 sermon at his son Franklin's crusade in Baltimore, at which he speculated that this would likely be the "last time" that he would speak to a crowd so large.

On August 14, 2006, *Newsweek* did a long tribute to him but caused a stir by touting Graham's "new thinking" about salvation. When asked whether Jews, Muslims, Buddhists, Hindus, or others will go to heaven, Graham replied: "Those are decisions only the Lord will make. It would be foolish for me to speculate on who will be there and who won't."

Ingrid Schlueter, an evangelical columnist and talk show host, said Graham's answer was a troubling deviation from Christian doctrine. She said that answering the *Newsweek* question directly didn't require speculation. "Why speculate," she said, "when you have the whole counsel of God in your hands and can declare the answer with authority? Has the man become a universalist?"[26]

Universalism is a doctrine that says God will ultimately save everyone, regardless of religious belief, because of his great mercy and grace. It is a doctrine that has traditionally been rejected by the Christian church, but one that has been increasingly creeping into evangelical circles. John Stott's book *Basic Christianity* was a must-read among young evangelicals in the 1970s. Later in life, however, he embraced the doctrine of annihilationism, which doesn't go so far as to say that everyone will be saved, but says that the souls of those who aren't saved will cease existing—be annihilated—when they die. Many theologians believe that, as a practical matter, universalism and annihilationism are the same thing. Both deny the need for Christ's sacrifice and the efficacy of God's grace.

It's not the first time the charge of universalism had been made against Graham. When Graham appeared on Robert Schuller's *Hour of Power* program in 1997, Schuller asked him about the future of Christianity, and Graham replied, "I think everybody that loves Christ, or knows Christ, whether they're conscious of it or not, they're members of the body of Christ. They may not even know the name of Jesus, but they know in their hearts that they need something that they don't have, and they turn to the only light that they have, and I think they are saved, and that they're going to be with us in heaven."[27]

When the *Newsweek* controversy erupted, Graham spokesman A. Larry Ross rescued the preacher. "As an evangelist for more than six decades, Mr. Graham has faithfully proclaimed the Bible's Gospel message that Jesus is the only way to Heaven," Ross said. He added: "However, salvation is the work of Almighty God, and only he knows what is in each human heart."

Graham himself has never retracted either statement.

Lies, More Lies, and Statistics

At the risk of piling on, let's look at one more example of how body-count evangelism has become both pervasive and perverting in modern evangelicalism, and that is in the megachurch.

Rick Warren is perhaps the most famous evangelical pastor in the United States, at least he was at the opening of the twenty-first century. He is the pastor of California's Saddleback Church. His church has grown to more than twenty thousand in weekly attendance, in part because of the phenomenal success of his book *The Purpose-Driven Life*, which sold more than twenty-five million copies. Warren has become, arguably, the most influential evangelical leader in the country, in many ways surpassing even Billy Graham. He writes often about church growth, leadership, and related issues. To help make a couple of points, I am going to quote extended passages from a column Warren wrote for the March 16, 2004, *Leadership Journal*.

> Three key responsibilities of every pastor are to discern where (and how) God's Spirit is moving in our culture and time, prepare your congregation for that movement, and cooperate with it to reach people Jesus died for. I call it "surfing spiritual waves" in *The Purpose-Driven Church*, and it's the reason Saddleback has grown to 23,500 on weekends in 24 years. . . . You don't criticize a wave; you just ride it as best you can.
>
> When Mel Gibson showed me his film, *The Passion of the Christ*, last year, I instantly thought of Jesus' words: "If I be lifted up I will draw all men unto me." That is his promise! Nothing is more magnetic than the power of the cross. So I knew a huge wave—a spiritual tsunami— would hit when the film debuted on February 25 [2004], and we began praying and preparing to surf it.

It's hard not to pause and explicate this passage in light of what we have discussed so far. The celebrity name-dropping, the appeal to size as an indication of God's blessing, the identification of an extrabiblical theory (spiritual waves) as a means of God's working—these are all theological and logical fallacies we have already discussed. This is the new provincialism, the triumph of sentimentality, and body-count evangelism all rolled up in a single paragraph.

Warren continued:

> First, we planned a two-part sermon series, "Understanding

the Passion," to bookend both sides of the movie's release. Next, we booked 47 theater screens for members to take their lost friends to. Third, Kay [Warren, Rick's wife] and I personally invited over a thousand lost community leaders of Orange County to a VIP premiere showing, including every mayor, congressman, superintendent of schools, other community leaders, and four billionaires, most of whom I'd never met. Then, in anticipation of all the lost friends brought by members, we added two more services to our regular weekend schedule of nine. Finally, we prepared a three-week small group curriculum on *The Passion* for follow-up.

The results? Over 600 unchurched community leaders attended our VIP showing; 892 friends of members were saved during the two-week sermon series. Over 600 new small groups were formed, and our average attendance increased by 3,000. That's catching a wave!

The problem with these numbers is that they cannot possibly be true. According to numbers the church itself reported to *Outreach* magazine, which compiles a list of the largest and fastest-growing churches in the United States, and which I examined in detail in an article for WORLD Magazine,[28] Saddleback's attendance probably fell during this period.

Warren wrote his article in *Leadership Journal* as a defense against those who criticized him for using *The Passion* as an evangelistic tool. In particular, he was responding to an article by Brian McLaren, who advocates an emergent church methodology to target young people. Warren spoke to McLaren directly when he concluded: "Many young pastors would be shocked to learn that the largest Gen-X church in America is Saddleback with over 20,000 names under 29 on our church roll."

Again, obviously these numbers cannot possibly be true. At the time Warren wrote this, it is likely that only about 21,000 people were attending his church. That would mean that virtually every person in the church was under the age of twenty-nine. (If that is true, the church has other problems.) But such are the perversions of truth of those who engage in body-count evangelism.

Some pastors are growing wise to these perversions of truth. Dan Burrell was the pastor of Northside Baptist Church in Charlotte, North Carolina, when *The Passion* came out. Its size—more than two thousand members—qualifies it for megachurch status. But Burrell says he has grown disillusioned with the efforts of the Christian-industrial complex to get him to participate in body-count evangelism. Interestingly, the movie *The Passion*, which provided the context for Rick Warren's article, also provided the context for Burrell's epiphany. Burrell wrote about the experience in a December 14, 2006, Evangelical Press News Service editorial he called "Pimpin' for Hollywood":

> I will admit that I got seduced into this a couple of years ago with Mel Gibson's "The Passion of the Christ." After having been given an "exclusive, pre-release" viewing limited to a few "personally invited and selected guests," I was convinced enough that it had evangelistic value that I bought out five screens at a local theatre before its public release and we

invited scores of non-believers to join us in watching the movie and discussing it afterwards. I recall one "decision," but no conversions, after all the effort and I learned my lesson. From that point forward, I've been pretty much immunized against "partnering" with Hollywood. Upon further reflection, I've reached the decision that pastors are actually being asked not to partner with, but to pimp for, Hollywood.

Burrell makes the important distinction between decisions and conversions, a distinction we have also made in our discussion. If that distinction seems a false one, consider this: The American Church Research Project reported that in 2000, only 18.7 percent of the U.S. population attended a Christian church on an average Sunday. That's about 52.5 million people. Ten years earlier, in 1990, that percentage was 20.4, or about 51 million. During that same decade, the number of megachurches in America more than doubled.[29]

That means claims by megachurch and seeker proponents that they are growing from the ranks of the unchurched are patently false. Simple mathematics rules out that possibility. There is no way megachurches can be growing at the rates they are without taking the overwhelming majority of their members from other churches.

The inescapable conclusion is this: the body of Christ is dying, or at least withering. It is not growing—at least here in the United States. An all but inescapable second conclusion is this: if the practitioners of body-count evangelism are not doing the killing, then they are at least standing by, enhancing their own power, watching those who are doing the stoning.

The Remains of the Day

In summary, we discuss body-count evangelism here because it is the logical consequence of the pathologies we have discussed so far: the new provincialism, the triumph of sentimentality, and the Christian-industrial complex. It produces this mindset: By any means available we will grow our numbers. When the most effective means are identified, we will reproduce them on a mass scale. Because we sincerely desire these large crowds to represent an enlargement in the body of Christ, or at least a genuine interest in spiritual matters, we will simply assume this to be so. We will never look back.

In the era of body-count evangelism, people become statistics. True salvations become opportunities not for joy, but for bragging. Consider, as an indictment of this worldview, the poignant comment from a woman who wrote me after the WORLD Magazine article came out unmasking some of the more egregious examples of body-count evangelism. She identified herself only as Jen:

> Twenty-eight years ago, I was a victim of "body-count evangelism." I was a trophy for someone, but not brought into the day-to-day presence of the humble, forgiving, suffering Christ. Didn't spend much time in conversation with God for a long time after that, except to carry around a load of shame.
>
> Many years later, I was supported by a community of deeply faithful and quietly eloquent fellow travelers. The faith I learned with them made no false promises,

didn't evaporate in the face of real life challenges, and—surprise, surprise—was completely consonant with the life and resurrection of Jesus. I have been in active ministry for nine years. I've had feedback that my life has encouraged a few people to get closer to God.

Numbers don't matter. Trust and depth of commitment and ability to communicate a transformed perspective—hearing these makes me rejoice. I know that there is sincerity in those who work for quantity and high-profile Christian recruiting (which is NOT evangelism), but I think it does a lot of damage. It did to me. And it adds a cultural obstacle to those of us who are trying to live out a servant's life. It takes a long time to establish trust with someone who has the other definition of "Christian" in their mind.

I trust you see that another theme is emerging in our discussion: community. The cure for the new provincialism is an awareness that we live in community with history. The cure for the Christian-industrial complex is a life in community with those who live around us—a community rooted in place. Jen points us toward the antidote for body-count evangelism, and once again it is a life in community, a true community of the Spirit.

CHAPTER 6

THE GREAT STEREOPTICON

The Church is to develop a realistic alternative to the contemporary technocracy which is marked by bondage, materialism, self-centredness, and greed. Christ's call to obedience is a call to be different, not conformist. Such a Church—joyful, obedient, loving, and free—will do more than please God: it will attract the world. It is when the Church evidently is the Church, and is living a supernatural life of love by the power of the Holy Spirit, that the world will believe.

    —JOHN R. W. STOTT IN *OBEYING CHRIST IN A CHANGING WORLD*

Technology emancipates not only from memory, but also from faith.

    —RICHARD WEAVER IN *IDEAS HAVE CONSEQUENCES*

The diseases we have discussed in the first five chapters might all fairly be described as pathologies of disengagement. We do not actively seek to be alienated, unloved and unloving, rootless, and confused. But this is precisely the condition in which we find ourselves when we reject the lessons and wisdom of history, when we allow sentimentality to triumph over reality, when we trade away community and vocation in favor of commerce, and when we desire trophies instead of converts.

Whether we disengage intentionally or not seems hardly to matter. C. S. Lewis, in his *Screwtape Letters*, wrote wisely and wryly on this point. In that book, a young demon—Wormwood—is charged with leading a human "patient" astray. He gets advice from his "affectionate uncle" Screwtape in a series of letters. At one point the human is seriously wrestling with God, and the young demon is panicky. He wants to send someone who will argue with his patient. Screwtape warns against that strategy, saying that the more effective strategy is not to engage his mind, but to disengage it. Here are excerpts from Screwtape's letter to the young fiend Wormwood:

> I once had a patient, a sound atheist, who used to read in the British Museum. One day, as he sat reading, I saw a train of thought in his mind beginning to go the wrong way. The Enemy, of course, was at his elbow in a moment. Before I knew where I was I saw my twenty years' work beginning to totter. If I had lost my head and begun to attempt a defence by argument I should have been undone. But I was not such a fool. I struck instantly at the part of the man which I had best under my control and suggested that it was just about time he had some lunch . . . .
>
> Do remember you are there to fuddle him. From the way some of you young fiends talk, anyone would suppose it was our job to teach![1]

Neil Postman, in *Amusing Ourselves to Death*, helps us to see that modern media are among the great "fuddlers" of all time. Postman wrote most of the book in the year 1984, when many culture critics were speculating on the degree to which the dark, totalitarian vision of George Orwell's *1984* had come to pass. But Postman said the world of 1984—and beyond, even to our present day—was not a reflection of Orwell's imagination so much as Aldous Huxley's *Brave New World*. Huxley feared not a totalitarian future, but a trivial one. In *Brave New World Revisited*, Huxley wrote about humankind's almost infinite appetite for distractions. Postman took up the argument: "'In *1984*,' Huxley added, 'people are controlled by inflicting pain. In *Brave New World*, they are controlled by inflicting pleasure.' In short, Orwell feared that what we hate will ruin us. Huxley feared that what we love will ruin us."[2]

The evangelical church has come to love modern media. The extent to which modern media—which I call *the great stereopticon*—has ruined or will ruin the church is the question we consider next.

The End Justifies the Medium

A. Larry Ross sat on a US Airways flight late at night, making the trip from Charlotte back to his home in Dallas. Ross is not a famous evangelical preacher like the men we have so far met: Billy Graham, Jerry Falwell, Rick Warren, and Bill Hybels. But all these men know (or knew) Ross. For years he was the chief public relations strategist for the Billy Graham Evangelistic Association. But he no longer works exclusively for Graham.

Several years before this mid-1990s flight, Ross had formed his own public relations agency, and now he represents some of the largest Christian ministries in the world.

It was just a coincidence that I was on this flight with him. I was headed for Dallas on completely unrelated business, but as a journalist who covered the Christian world, I immediately recognized him. For one thing, Ross stands over six and a half feet tall. For another, while most everyone else on this nighttime flight was sleeping, Ross was demonstrating the work ethic that made him arguably one of the top PR guys in the world. Though he had to all but fold himself up to get in his coach seat, he was still able to lower the tray table and spread out some papers on this late-night flight.

In front of him was the slick media kit for the Christian band dcTalk. Though the members of the band had graduated from Jerry Falwell's Liberty University, the trio of two white guys and a black guy—and their mastery of rap with Christian lyrics—was still considered a bit edgy in the evangelical Christian world. So the decision by the Graham organization to use the band in its crusades for its Saturday-night youth nights involved some risk. After all, there had been recent scandals in the Christian music world. Superstar Sandi Patti had just been through a messy divorce, causing many (though not all) Christian radio stations to yank her music from the airwaves. Michael English, a former member of the iconic Gaither Vocal Band and then a solo artist with a soaring and distinctive voice, had just admitted an extramarital affair with another Christian artist, as well as drug use.

Ross, more than any other person, knew how important it was for the evangelical world to have its own stars, its heroes. Ross would say that Jesus should always be the real star, but making a few human stars would bring out the crowds; and these crowds could then be introduced to Jesus. At least that was the idea.

But as the Christian market grew, the star-making machinery put pressures on the artists that were almost too great for humans to bear, thus the fall of Patti and English—and, for that matter, Jimmy Swaggart and Jim Bakker. Some Christian artists—as we have already suggested—openly rebelled against what the Christian music industry was becoming: the Christian-industrial complex.

One of these stories is particularly instructive. In the early 1980s, Leslie Phillips burst onto the Christian music scene and was being billed as the "Christian Cyndi Lauper." But as her artistic sensibilities ran in a different direction from the one her handlers wanted, conflicts arose and so did the pressure. That pressure found an outlet artistically and romantically with producer T-Bone Burnett, who left his wife to marry Phillips.

Phillips ended up leaving the world of Christian music and leaving in a huff, going public with her complaints about the Christian-industrial complex that tried to force her to compromise her artistic integrity for the sake of a pop image. But many of the people in the Christian world saw her as a homewrecker because of her affair with Burnett, so her often-valid criticisms were seen as rationalizations and sour grapes. She changed her name to Sam Phillips and continued to have a successful music career outside of the Christian music world. For two decades she has remained publicly silent about her time in Christian music. She and Burnett divorced in 2004.

Of course, these sorts of stories abound in the secular world. But there is an important difference. If a country artist gets divorced, it becomes the subject of his (or her) next album. If a secular rap artist gets busted for drugs and goes to jail for a time, he earns "street cred," credibility on the urban streets where his music is actually being bought and played. If the same things happen to Christian artists, their careers are over, and all those around them—the record companies, the ministry partners, the management, all those who depend on them for cash—have a big problem. The cash spigot turns off almost instantly as Christian radio stations and Christian bookstores yank their records, and there is rarely any coming back.

So Ross and the Graham team would check out dcTalk carefully before using them. But use them they did. Because they knew that they were communicating in a medium—rap music—that kids were listening to. And if there is one fundamental idea of modern evangelicalism that trumps all others, it is that method, techniques, and technology are morally and theologically neutral. That idea is often expressed in this way: It doesn't matter how you communicate the gospel. Any method will work so long as you don't change the message.

But is this statement, in fact, true? Are media neutral? By now you should have a healthy skepticism, at least regarding that question. In this chapter we will attempt to give that skepticism a solid place to stand.

Decomposed Eternity

When Richard Weaver wrote *Ideas Have Consequences* in the 1940s, he knew that something new was happening. It was the advent of the television age. Weaver recognized in this new medium something fundamentally different from all previous media, even radio. That difference is the combination of words, sound, and pictures, which attempts to create a kind of "decomposed eternity," that is, an impression that suggests permanence but vanishes as soon as it appears. But he also knew that television wasn't "the thing"; it was just the current manifestation of "the thing." That's why his criticism wasn't aimed at television, per se, but at what he called "the great stereopticon," which was a prescient way of describing the convergence of media into a common idiom long before the word *convergence* became a standard part of the digital age's lexicon.

Neil Postman, in *Amusing Ourselves to Death*, came to many of the same conclusions about modern media that combine words, sound, and images. First of all, he acknowledged that what Weaver called the stereopticon really is something entirely different. It is not just an incremental shift or improvement, but a new species. Postman said that there have been only a few true paradigm shifts in the history of human discourse. The first was the advent of speech. Speech is perhaps humankind's most distinguishing characteristics, which is why Postman called it the "primal and indispensable medium."[3]

Of course, the Judeo-Christian tradition understands God as the creator of speech. First, as Creator, God spoke the world into existence. Second, one of God's first instructions to Adam was to name the animals. In this command God gave humans the gift of speech. But there's more to this gift than just the ability to speak; it is also the gift to see "the truth of things," once again to borrow the expression from Thomas Aquinas. When God commanded Adam to name the animals, he was, in effect, telling us that he had given us the capacity to see the true nature of the world. This story, not incidentally, is at the core of any biblical argument against nihilism and relativism, because it teaches us that reality exists and that it is knowable and nameable.

According to Postman, the widespread use of the written word was the next great shift. This shift from the spoken word to the written word also had a monumental impact on culture, because written speech allowed the codification of common beliefs and the organization of nations. Rulers could govern by edict and law, which allowed a ruler's influence to extend well beyond the sound of his voice.

Postman said that the next great media development came with movable type, which once again wrought many dramatic innovations. Perhaps the most significant cultural shifts that followed hard on the heels of the invention of movable type were the Renaissance, revolutionizing the world of art and culture, and the Reformation, which transformed the world of religion. And just a short time after that, the Enlightenment brought change in the worlds of politics and science.

These changes came about in part because knowledge could be decentralized. Books—which could be created cheaply and transported efficiently—made not just literacy but also advanced study a real possibility for all of humanity. And though this idea is beyond the scope of this book, it could be argued that this great decentralization is the story of the modern world. In religion, we see church polity, or governance, devolve from "one holy, catholic, and apostolic church" to the Great Schism that divided East and West and then to the Presbyterian and congregational denominations following the Reformation. In government we see the devolution of power from kings to the people.[4]

Likewise, history tells us of a great cultural hegemony emanating from southern Europe. This hegemony had its roots in Christendom, most especially in the Roman Catholic Church, and then manifested itself in the Renaissance. This emanation northward throughout Europe and then across the ocean to America was largely due to a technological innovation: movable type made the movement of ideas and the education of large masses of people less complicated. The basic facts (or at least the chronology) of the Renaissance followed by the Reformation followed by the Enlightenment are well known to most schoolchildren. However, we don't often pause to note how remarkable it is that the "center of the known world" could reside within a few hundred miles of the Tigris and Euphrates rivers for thousands of years—first in Egypt, then in Greece, and then in Rome—but in the space of just a few hundred years following the invention of movable type, the entire world shifted on its axis across a continent, an ocean, and many languages.

Is it any wonder, then, that the rise of the great stereopticon would also create its own huge cultural and religious shift, generating previously unknown and unintended consequences? This ability to blend sound, image, and word is only just now coming into full flower, and it is obvious to many that it is the kind of shift that has happened only a few times in history. We marvel that through television hundreds of millions of us can watch our first steps on the moon or that we can have the sense that "we are all New Yorkers" because we can see in real time the collapse of the World Trade Center towers.

But we would be foolish, or at least shortsighted, if we did not acknowledge the other side of the coin. And the other side of the coin is this: it is also clear that the great stereopticon has great destructive power. It produces isolation, despair, and disintegration of spirit. We have to go no further than the examples I cited above. Neil Armstrong was the first man on the moon, not I. We are not all New Yorkers—unless, of course, we are. My point is that these television images made us feel something, but that something is something that we are not. It is terribly easy for that which we feel about ourselves to be mistaken for that which is true about ourselves.

But it is not true. It is false.

And the real question is this: Is this tendency of the great stereopticon to tell lies about reality the result of its abuse and misuse, or is it the inevitable and unavoidable consequence of its use? In other words, does the great stereopticon inevitably pervert whatever message that goes into it? Before we answer that question, let's establish that it is indeed worth asking and answering by highlighting the ubiquity of the great stereopticon in the church.

The Evangelical Church and the Great Stereopticon

By some measures the great stereopticon has become the primary communication tool of the evangelical church.

Christian television is perhaps the most obvious example of the great stereopticon at work in the evangelical world, and the rise of Christian television corresponds, not coincidentally, with the rise of the postwar evangelical movement. Radio had paved the way. In fact, you could argue that the first radio broadcast was a Christian broadcast. Wireless broadcasts of Morse code had been around since the late nineteenth century, but an engineer named Reginald Fessenden devised a microphone that had the ability to convert sounds into the same electrical impulses. On Christmas Eve 1906 Fessenden made a short broadcast from the Brant Rock, Massachusetts, wireless station. For several days before, he had used Morse code to tell wireless operators to be listening. And when the time came, he hooked up his crude "spark-gap" microphone and began a short broadcast. He played a portion of Handel's "Largo," using an Edison wax cylinder machine. He explained what he was doing and how. Then he played a portion of "O Holy Night" on the violin. He concluded his broadcast by wishing all a merry Christmas and reciting a verse from the Christmas story: "Glory to God in the highest. On earth peace to men of good will."[5]

The event shocked wireless operators on U.S. Navy ships at sea and at wireless stations as far south as Norfolk, Virginia, the eventual home of the Christian Broadcasting Network.

163

The age of broadcasting had begun. And churches and denominations were in on it from the beginning. Mark Ward wrote an authorized history of Christian broadcasting for the National Religious Broadcasters (NRB) on the occasion of its fiftieth anniversary in 1994. He wrote that *The Lutheran Hour* with Walter A. Maier and the *Old Fashioned Revival Hour* with Charles E. Fuller both had audiences in the millions by the 1940s. According to Ward, "Fuller was the biggest name on the Mutual Broadcasting Network," the network that gave Walter Cronkite his start. At its peak in 1943, Fuller's program was spending nearly thirty thousand dollars a week to purchase airtime. This at a time when a middle-class home could be purchased for four thousand dollars and many U.S. families lived on less than two thousand dollars a year. Indeed, Fuller's *Old Fashioned Revival Hour* bought "50 percent more airtime than the next largest secular customer. Altogether, the Mutual network received more than one-fourth of its revenues from religious broadcasters."[6]

But television was the next big thing. NBC's first station went on the air in New York in 1930, but television was a novelty until Franklin Roosevelt stood before the camera to open the 1939 New York World's Fair. The interest of the public and station license applications soared. In 1941 the Federal Communications Commission (FCC) ruled that television broadcasters could accept advertising, and that should have set in motion a land rush of new stations; but World War II intervened. For the next four years, the FCC issued no licenses, and the production of new television sets was banned so that all possible manufacturing capabilities could be focused on the war effort.

The freeze in station licenses turned out, though, to be a blessing in disguise for the fledgling industry. Wartime research and development were quickly translated into peacetime capabilities. If the FCC had been granting licenses from 1941 through 1945, the result would have been a chaotic mess of incompatible and competing technologies. But when the FCC adopted industry standards in 1947, the marketplace had already pretty much decided what they would be. With a single standard, the number of televisions in U.S. homes grew at nothing less than a geometric rate.

In 1947 there were only fifty thousand television sets in use in the entire country. By 1948, just a year later, fifty thousand sets were being sold each month.

The NRB says that *Lutheran Hour*'s Walter Maier gets the prize for preaching the "first nondenominational worship service ever seen on television," in 1948. But an even more interesting date, for our purposes, is November 5, 1950—the first television broadcast of the Billy Graham Evangelistic Association, carried by ABC on 150 stations.

That first broadcast took place two days before the midterm elections. Republicans made gains in both houses that year, "shaving the Democratic majority in the Senate from twelve to two and in the House from seventeen to twelve," wrote Whitaker Chambers's biographer Sam Tanenhaus.[7] Tanenhaus identified one "conspicuous winner" among the Republicans, a man Graham had met during his long crusade in California, the one the Hearst newspapers had been so instrumental in promoting. That conspicuous winner was the staunchly anticommunist Richard Nixon. Though Graham says that in those days he was registered as a Democrat, some say Graham should get some of the credit for Nixon's success. Nixon's hard-edged anticommunism and a personal style that was not warm were off-putting to many. Nixon's association with Graham, who was beginning to appear on annual surveys of "most admired people," helped soften Nixon's image.

Indeed, some say Graham's association with Republican politicians was the seed for what came to be a decades-long association between Republicans and religious conservatives.

Because our purpose here is not to recount the entire history of Christian broadcasting, I will observe only that the rise of television also more or less corresponds with the rise of parachurch ministries. Campus Crusade for Christ, Navigators, InterVarsity Christian Fellowship, Young Life, World Vision, the Billy Graham Evangelistic Association, and scores of other ministries were founded near the end of World War II. And, of course, as techniques and methodologies were developed and perfected— especially fund-raising techniques—ministries such as Focus on the Family, the American Family Association, Trinity Broadcasting Network, the PTL Network, the Inspiration Networks, and many others were almost exclusively media based.

In other words, it is fair to say that the modern parachurch, for better or worse, would not exist as it does today without the great stereopticon.

The Great Stereopticon
Becomes the Church

But the use of media as an outreach tool is only a part of the story of the great stereopticon and the evangelical church. Perhaps even more significant is the use of media in worship.

In a 2005 survey by Christian pollster George Barna, more than six out of ten Protestant churches (62 percent) used a large-screen projection system in their worship services.[8] Just five years earlier, in 2000, only 39 percent used this technology. A 2003 survey by the Calvin Institute of Christian Worship studied the use of video technology in worship and returned similar data. The Calvin Institute study speculated that less than 25 percent used projections in 1998.[9]

Clearly, the use of video in worship has spread dramatically. Advocates and critics alike agree that projection equipment has totally changed the nature of worship services. What is interesting is that given the tremendous interest in the effects of television on the culture in general, the evangelical church has embraced the technology rapidly and almost completely uncritically. Consider, by way of contrast, that some version of the pipe organ has existed since the second century BC, but it was not until the thirteenth century that it came into common use in churches and cathedrals. In other words, the church has often been slow to adopt new technology—and wisely so, as we have seen, because the true impact of new technology is often profound and not immediately seen in the culture. But that has not been the case with video technology, which was adopted by churches rapidly and with little discussion of its impact on either worship or the community life of the congregation.

Also, advocates for new technology in the church have successfully neutered their critics. They have reduced the criticism of new technology to arguments over taste and style and have ignored arguments related to theology or effect. And, to be sure, the critics of new technology have not made their case very effectively, often focusing on matters of taste, style, or a vague appeal to the wisdom of history and tradition.

Taste and style issues are important, because ultimately they relate to conceptions of beauty. And beauty, as Thomas Aquinas teaches us, is the "mediation of the good." Aquinas also believed that the "three formal characters of beauty" are clarity, integrity, and proportion.[10] In signifying integrity as an essential characteristic of beauty, Aquinas was saying that which is beautiful must also be true. Art, or any abstract signification of reality, which certainly includes our methods of worship and teaching, must maintain fidelity to the thing being represented.

So arguments based on taste and style are not without merit, but to modern sensibilities they rarely carry the day. Neither do arguments based on history and tradition, which the new provincialism has rendered unintelligible to modern minds—however true. They seem obtuse and arcane, even to the intellectually sophisticated.

But the real problem with these arguments about taste and style or even about history and tradition is a problem that I acknowledge: without linking them to philosophical or theological presuppositions, they remain subjective. That is the fallacy that those on both sides of the worship wars tend to commit. And the result is that both sides begin to talk in a code that the other side does not accept as valid. Traditionalists might argue that something is in poor taste or "kitschy" or too loud. They may even argue that it is irreverent or worldly. Those on the other side argue that the traditional worship styles are boring or irrelevant or even meaningless. But these arguments have lost the power to convince, because neither side accepts the presuppositions of the other.

That is why I want to leave aside, at least temporarily, questions of style and taste and examine some of the best thinking we've been able to produce about the true nature of the great stereopticon.

Amusing Ourselves to Death

Neil Postman devoted a chapter in *Amusing Ourselves to Death* to televangelists, mainly Jim Bakker and Jimmy Swaggart. Because of the scandals surrounding these two, they did not fare well in Postman's treatment. But Postman's criticism of television preachers was not limited to those involved in scandal. In fact, he seems to suggest that the mendacity of these preachers was to be expected. He suggested that it is integral to their daily deconstruction of reality, their intentional and necessary intellectual disengagement—a disengagement that the electronic media both allow and require. Postman wrote: "No clearer example of the difference between earlier and modern forms of public discourse can be found than in the contrast between the theological arguments of Jonathan Edwards and those of, say,

Jerry Falwell, or Billy Graham, or Oral Roberts. The formidable content to Edwards' theology must inevitably engage the intellect; if there is such a content to the theology of the television evangelicals, they have not yet made it known."[11]

This disengagement with the intellect and theology, Postman asserted, is the inevitable "difference between the character of discourse in a print-based culture and the character of discourse in a television-based culture."[12]

You may remember that earlier we asked if media were morally neutral. In other words, is there a morally or spiritually preferred medium? Postman did not answer that question, but he did assert that media necessarily shape a message and that some media are more appropriate than others for communicating some messages. Postman observed, for example, that it is impossible to communicate philosophy using smoke signals. Smoke signals could, however, communicate my presence and my desire to communicate. If signals could be agreed on by some other means, a primitive intellectual commerce could be continued. But that's about it.

Postman also maintained that all new media necessarily, inevitably, have positive and negative cultural effects. For example, the development of the alphabet and a written language—innovations universally accepted as positive developments in the history of civilization—nonetheless had a detrimental effect on oral tradition. Postman therefore asserted that poetry thrives in an oral culture. Fiction, law, and philosophy thrive in a written culture. Entertainment thrives in a video culture. And by *thrive* he meant dominate. He meant thrive as kudzu thrives in parts of the South—by killing everything else in its habitat.

Postman is no Luddite. He is not opposed to the use of technology. But he maintains, as did Hawthorne when discussing the plight of the writer or any artist, that there is a "devil in the inkpot." The lesson in this, according to Postman, is that because all new media have a negative effect, the path of wisdom is to understand the net effect of new technology. That which the new technology would destroy must be intentionally preserved. Otherwise it will be lost indeed.

The Medium Is the Message

An even more famous figure in the development of our understanding of modern media, the great stereopticon, is Marshall McLuhan.

McLuhan's famous phrase, "the medium is the message," is more often quoted than understood, in part because McLuhan himself—a great purveyor of pithy witticisms and sound bites—was more subtle and nuanced in his ideas than the very sound bites he was known for.[13] McLuhan never said that the content of the message is irrelevant, only that content has a "distinctly subordinate" impact. It is the medium, the technology, that has the real impact. It's worth taking a look at an extended quote from McLuhan from an interview he did with *Playboy* magazine.

> *PLAYBOY:* Even if, as you contend, the medium is the ultimate message, how can you entirely discount the importance of content? Didn't the content of Hitler's radio speeches, for example, have some effect on the Germans?
>
> McLuHAN: By stressing that the medium is the message

rather than the content, I'm not suggesting that content plays no role—merely that it plays a distinctly subordinate role. Even if Hitler had delivered botany lectures, some other demagogue would have used the radio to retribalize the Germans and rekindle the dark atavistic side of the tribal nature that created European fascism in the Twenties and Thirties. By placing all the stress on content and practically none on the medium, we lose all chance of perceiving and influencing the impact of new technologies on man, and thus we are always dumfounded by—and unprepared for—the revolutionary environmental transformations induced by new media. Buffeted by environmental changes he cannot comprehend, man echoes the last plaintive cry of his tribal ancestor, Tarzan, as he plummeted to earth: "Who greased my vine?" The German Jew victimized by the Nazis because his old tribalism clashed with their new tribalism could no more understand why his world was turned upside down than the American today can understand the reconfiguration of social and political institutions caused by the electric media in general and television in particular.[14]

A new technology revolutionizes an environment. One of McLuhan's favorite examples has come to be known as "McLuhan's light bulb." Imagine a dark room. What are the contents of the room? It's impossible to know. What is your behavior in the room? Is it determined by the room's content or by the room's darkness? Both, of course, but much more so by the darkness, as becomes obvious when the light goes on. When the light comes on, the contents of the room might seem new and surprising or threatening and dangerous or exactly what you expected. But in reality the content had not changed. Only the medium changed. Darkness became light.

McLuhan said that television's effects are particularly radical in their ability to reshape the environment, because they "suspend judgment." This ability of television (and movies) is different from what Coleridge called the "willing suspension of disbelief" necessary for a reader to enter into a work of fiction or the conceit of a poem. The primary difference is precisely that with the written word, the suspension of disbelief is, in fact, willing. It is not compelled in the way that video images compel.

McLuhan said it this way: "Any technology tends to create a new human environment. Technological environments are not merely passive containers of people but are active processes that reshape people and other technologies alike."[15]

The Moviegoer

Perhaps the most brilliant dramatization in all of literature of the relationship of the great stereopticon to its dislocating, alienating effects is Walker Percy's first novel, the National Book Award–winning *The Moviegoer*.

The book's protagonist is Binx Bolling. Bolling is a young, moderately successful stockbroker who is depressed, alienated, and alone. Despite his affluence, education, and accomplishments, he has an inkling that his life is trivial and banal. Rather than directly confront that inkling and turn it into a fully formed diagnosis, he escapes that difficult intellectual and spiritual struggle by going to the movies. He observes his life by analogy. An experience he has will be "like William Holden" in a movie he had just seen. Bolling will say a woman is as "extinguished in her soul as Eva Marie Saint."

Percy also penetrated the modernist's need for celebrity, the need of the everyday people to validate their existence by being in the presence of, or at least in the orbit of, celebrities, be they television preachers or movie stars. Critic John Murphy wrote of *The Moviegoer:*

> Being "Somewhere" and being "Someone" informs Binx's search. Bolling observes another young man's chance encounter with William Holden, star of celluloid classics like *Sunset Boulevard* and *Bridge on the River Kwai.* When Holden pats the fellow's shoulder in a gesture of camaraderie, Bolling thinks, "The boy has done it! He has won title to his own existence." Binx has attributed to Holden what Christians attribute to God—the ability to affirm one's existence. Thus, for Binx, the movie theater has replaced the church as a place of worship. This substitution is at the heart of Binx's malaise. The cathedral is a place to celebrate humanity redeemed by a God who is Love. A movie theater is a place to escape humanity by watching, without participating, reduced and artificial visions of humanity.[16]

Walker Percy believed in the role of the novelist as diagnostician. In other words, the role of the artist is to rightly name the disease of his times. Only in the right naming of the disease could a cure be properly prescribed. Though Percy was a Roman Catholic with a well-developed apprehension of Puritanism, he was in this particularity—the naming of the malaise, or the sin, of his time—a blood brother to Jonathan Edwards.

A part of what is remarkable about all of this analysis I have offered about the great stereopticon is that it is generally accepted as true, especially by Christians. When this analysis is offered as a critique on the mainstream news media, for example, it elicits a hearty "Amen!" We understand the alienating, soul-numbing effects of the great stereopticon, yet for some reason—or for many reasons—we pretend that the great stereopticon does not have the same effect on our worship. We witness the cult of celebrity that surrounds our preachers. We witness the rise of the megachurch and the parachurch and the commensurate erosion of community and accountability. We not only witness these phenomena but also nurture them. It is now common that a new church's first home is the local movie cineplex. A growing megachurch innovation is not to plant new churches at all, but to clone themselves as a multisite church. The people gather, but much of the service—the sermon, in particular—is broadcast from the main campus.

All of these innovations have been accepted uncritically by the evangelical church. For the most part, we now accept them without alloy or irony—or any effort to intentionally build in or replace what these innovations inevitably destroy in terms of community or accountability. The result is that we have seen the transformative power of faithful self-reflection and community dissipated to the point that the lifestyles of Christians are indistinguishable from non-Christians in important ways. We see all of these harmful effects and say, "Yes, but we are different." To modernize Hawthorne's "devil in the inkpot" metaphor, we say this: "Yes, the devil in the great stereopticon has possessed others, but we are immune from its effects."

It is a conclusion that should now seem—at the very least—implausible.

Context Matters

In this chapter I have tried to make the case that media are neither morally neutral nor culturally neutral. The impact of the great stereopticon is both powerful and pervasive. It changes all that it touches. It is like light or gravity in that the object of its power determines only slightly the impact. Dark objects might absorb more light or lighter objects might exert less pull, but it is the reality of the light and the gravity, and not the size or color of the object, that determines the ultimate effect.

There is one other consideration we should examine before we offer an answer to the question that we started with: Does Scripture dictate a preferred medium for the communication of the gospel? And that issue is context.

In the introduction to this book, I shared with you a plausible but fictional story to demonstrate the importance of context to the communication of content. In that story, I said that the message "Fear not. Jesus is Lord." might be unchanged from one medium to the next. However, that message has one effect when it is spoken by a televangelist asking for your money and quite another effect when it is spoken by a beloved pastor comforting you in a time of grave sickness. The words may be exactly the same, but the messages could not be more different.

I learned this lesson when I was in high school with a girl who would eventually become a world-class musician. Jennifer Larmore is a name well known to opera lovers. She is one of the world's best-known mezzo-sopranos, having portrayed Carmen and many other notable lead characters on some of the great stages of the world and for many years has been a regular with New York's Metropolitan Opera.

But before all that, Jenny Larmore was a classmate of mine at Sprayberry High School in Marietta, Georgia, and once we were competitors in our school's talent contest. I was playing trombone in a jazz ensemble that could really rip through Glenn Miller's "In the Mood." Indeed, we thought we had a decent chance of winning the contest, especially when we heard that Jenny, whom we knew even then to be enormously talented, was going to perform nothing more adventurous than the Lennon-McCartney chestnut "Yesterday."

But when it came Jenny's time to perform, the floor of the gymnasium, which was our makeshift stage, was totally darkened. Jenny came to the middle of the floor and stood next to the microphone in the dark. A single, tightly focused spot caused her face to light up like the moon as the familiar introduction to the song started ringing through the room. Her voice rang out clearly: "Yesterday, all my troubles seemed so far away."

But, slowly, the spot enlarged, and it was clear that sweet, young Jenny, perhaps foreshadowing the dramatic sensibilities that would make her an electrifying Carmen, was in costume. As the spot enlarged, it was obvious that this was not Jenny Larmore singing an easy-listening standard, but a young woman dressed up to be nine-months pregnant, with her hands resting on her distended midsection. We sat in stunned silence as she sang the second line: "Now it looks as though they're here to stay." And by the time she got to the second verse—"Suddenly, he's not half the man he used to be"—we were over our shock, and the look of comic disgust on Jenny's face as she sang that line and looked down at her belly brought the house down.

It was only later that I reflected on the fact that Jenny's voice was in perfect control throughout the performance. She varied not one syllable from the melancholy, nostalgic lines that Lennon and McCartney had written. But her performance of this song had totally changed the message. It became a rich and sophisticated comedy. She retired from the stage to a standing ovation. Jenny won the talent contest that year. (If I remember correctly, our jazz ensemble came in second.)

I didn't know it then, but what I witnessed that night was proof that Marshall McLuhan was right: the medium really is the message. When you change the medium, you change the message, whether you intend to or not and though the words remain exactly the same. It is a lesson the evangelical church has not yet learned.

The Foolishness of Preaching

So, if media are not neutral, does God have a preferred medium?

If the Bible is your guide, the answer to that question is yes. Paul's point in 1 Corinthians 1:20–23 is explicit: "Where is the wise man? Where is the scholar? Where is the philosopher of this age? Has not God made foolish the wisdom of the world? For since in the wisdom of God the world through its wisdom did not know him, God was pleased through the foolishness of what was preached to save those who believe. Jews demand miraculous signs and Greeks look for wisdom, but we preach Christ crucified: a stumbling block to Jews and foolishness to Gentiles."

Words—and not pictures, drama, or any other medium— seem to be the preferred strategy of God, of Jesus, and of Scripture. The Bible is not a picture book, and it well could have been, since much of it was written at times and in cultures when pictographs and hieroglyphics were common. Neil Postman believes that the use of words was an intentional strategy. "The God of the Jews was to exist in the word and through the word," Postman observed, and he explained why: words require the "highest level of abstract thinking."[17]

The observation that words require a high level of abstract thinking is an extraordinarily important idea and one that is easy to validate in our own experience. I and many millions more were fans of J. R. R. Tolkien's *The Lord of the Rings* long before it was made into a movie. Several of the characters, Gandalf and Aragorn in particular, made strong impressions on me when I first read the books as a teenager. I had strong mental pictures of them that I constructed when I met them on the page and adjusted as I learned more about them. Now, however, I can scarcely remember those images because when I think of Gandalf, I see

Ian McKellan, the actor who played Gandalf. Likewise, when I remember Aragorn, I see Viggo Mortensen in my mind's eye.

This is a common experience. Indeed, it is an inevitable experience, demonstrating the power of the great stereopticon. It is one of the reasons some rock bands at first resisted music videos: they dictate images to the hearer of the song.[18]

The Myth of Postmodernism

Those who advocate the myth of postmodernism say that something has happened in our culture. However you define modernism, that era has ended. We now live in a post-modern age. They argue that to postmoderns truth doesn't matter and that logical arguments are no longer persuasive. Further, they say that if Jesus were alive today, he would be using all the tools of the modern media to communicate the gospel. Emergent church guru Brian McLaren (and others) maintains that young people raised in a media age no longer respond to—or treat with irony or mythologizing—rational argument, to invitations to "come now, let us reason together."

They say, whether intentionally or not, that God and the fundamental nature of people have changed.

It's important to point out first and foremost the self-contradictory nature of that argument. The advocates of postmodernism have still not found a better way than words, facts, data, and rational argument to claim that words, facts, data, and rational arguments lack efficacy. Their own dialectical strategies are the best arguments against the position they advocate.

Second, claiming that Jesus would have used modern media if he were living on earth today demonstrates the cultural arrogance of the new provincialism. It argues that the culture of today is superior to the cultures of the past—specifically the culture in which Jesus lived. It was, by the way, the argument the Judas character made in the '70s rock opera *Jesus Christ Superstar*. Judas sang: "If you came today you could have reached the entire nation. Israel in 4 BC had no mass communication." Indeed, by putting those words in the mouth of the man who betrayed Jesus, they possess a powerful irony. The problem today is that evangelical leaders presume to give Jesus the same advice the Judas character gave, and the irony is lost.

David Wells, in his classic *No Place for Truth: Whatever Happened to Evangelical Theology?*, put the matter succinctly: "But biblical faith is about truth. God has described himself and his works to us in the language of the Bible, and it is quite presumptuous for us to say that we have found a better way to hear him and a better way to find reality."[19]

Third, dependence on the great stereopticon and rejection of the "foolishness of preaching" deny the Word of God itself. God promised: "My word . . . will not return to me empty, but will accomplish what I desire and achieve the purpose for which I sent it" (Isaiah 55:11). We cannot ignore the power of the Word of God any more than we can ignore gravity. When the Word of God is faithfully preached, as in Jonathan Edwards's day, it bears fruit. But back in chapter one, we began our discussion by making visible the myth of evangelical growth. We came to the conclusion that, in fact, the evangelical church as a whole is not bearing fruit, either numerically or spiritually. So what conclusion can we draw from that? There are only two possibilities: either the Word of God has lost its power, or it is not being faithfully proclaimed. I would suggest that if our work is not bearing fruit, it is not because the Word of God has lost its power. It can only be because we are no longer faithfully preaching it.

Fourth, the postmodern worldview, with its dependence on the great stereopticon, comes dangerously close, once again, to denying the incarnation of Christ. We mentioned earlier that one of the reasons the new provincialism, the denial of history, is such a grievous error is that the denial of history denies the God of history. God chooses to work in history. At times of his own choosing, he intervenes in history. His most conspicuous intervention is the incarnation, the coming of Jesus. When we submit to the postmodern myth and bow to the idol of the great stereopticon, with its deconstructed reality, we again show our disdain for the God of the incarnation. We seek again to "be like God."

It is the ultimate triumph of sentimentality.

CHAPTER 7

CHRISTIANITY'S NEXT SMALL THING

No system or machinery or . . . theory stands on its own feet: it is invariably
built on a metaphysical foundation, that is to say, upon man's basic outlook
on life, its meaning and purpose.

　—E. F. SCHUMACHER IN *SMALL IS BEAUTIFUL*

Learn from me, for I am gentle and humble in heart.

　—JESUS IN MATTHEW 11:29

So far, we have identified the fact that something has gone
wrong with evangelicalism—from sea to shining sea, as Thomas
McGuane put it (in a different context)—and suggested that
what has gone wrong is distinctly American in invention.

And in case the point of the argument has been lost in the
argument itself, let us now say it directly: virtually no part of

the American religious experience has remained unravaged by the overwhelming systems and machinery we have discussed. Indeed, not only has the body of Christ been seduced by the sentimentality and existentialism of modernism, but we are also being fully prostituted by it.

Given our current state, is recovery possible? The short answer to that question is yes. Indeed, that is the nature of God's grace: there is no condition outside of its reach. On a more practical level we might ask the question this way: Is anyone getting it right? Some are. And that is where we next turn, on this the third and last stage of our journey together, this chapter and the next, where we talk about where the trailhead for the path back might be.

Having Quite Lost My Way, I Came to Myself

Thomas W. Johnston Jr. ("T. J.") was not, in 1984, a guy you would have picked out of a crowd as a likely candidate to work among the poor in Haiti. But here he was, three years later, in 1987, in downtown Port-au-Prince, working in an office with no air conditioning and iron bars on the windows. From time to time gunshots could be heard. Indeed, a coup d'etat was under way, one of several that had occurred since Johnston had arrived in Haiti a year before. Gunfire, especially at night, was common. Johnston said one day he was sitting in his office and a bullet ricocheted in, bounced off the ceiling, and landed on his desk in front of him. He put the spent bullet in his top desk drawer and kept working.

This was a long way from the Kappa Alpha house at Sewanee, where Johnston (my brother-in-law) hung out during his college years, less than a decade earlier. Sewanee, as the University of the South is commonly called, is a venerable school perched high on the Cumberland Plateau in eastern Tennessee, modeled in architecture and pedagogy after England's Oxford University.

The school was and is an Episcopal stronghold—both for better and for worse, given the ups and downs of that denomination. And whatever else that might mean, it is fair to say that Sewanee is about as far away from the low-church evangelicalism of the southern countryside that surrounds it as you can possibly get and still be called Christian. Indeed, for many at Sewanee, the word *Christian* itself barely still applied. Though Sewanee is an undergraduate college, it has one graduate program: theology. The Episcopal seminary at Sewanee has become one of the most liberal in the country despite its rural, southern setting. In fact, it was at Sewanee, many believed, that a wry expression originated: "The Episcopal Church is the perfect church, because it interferes neither with a man's politics nor his religion."

There was another notorious expression popular at Sewanee, infamous for its drinking culture: "Where you find four Episcopalians, you will find a fifth." It was in this environment that T. J. Johnston matriculated, and upon graduation he attended law school in Birmingham, Alabama. He ultimately became partner in the largest law firm in Charleston, South Carolina. By the time he was thirty years of age, Johnston had a beautiful wife and two thriving children, a six-figure income, a house on Sullivan's Island, an affluent beach community just across the

Cooper River Causeway from his downtown Charleston office—and very little contact with the poor.

But in 1984 images from the Ethiopian famine exploded on television screens all across America. The city of Charleston, and many other cities, organized a community-wide relief effort. The city raised enough money to fill up a Boeing 747 with food and other relief items. But because of a rampant black market in Ethiopia, the city fathers said someone should accompany the flight. Johnston volunteered. By night he stayed in a luxury hotel in Addis Ababa. But by day he was ferried into the countryside where he saw children die before his very eyes. He saw teenagers so emaciated and small from years of malnourishment that they looked like infants, too dehydrated to cry real tears, many with intravenous feeding tubes coming out of their heads because the blood vessels in their scalps were the only ones healthy enough to take a needle.

Several years later, Johnston told the story, standing on the edge of Port-au-Prince's notorious City Soleil slum. He described how his growing faith in Jesus and what he had seen in Ethiopia came together in a single moment that he summed up this way: "Practicing law suddenly seemed absurd to me."

Johnston's story is in some ways archetypal. It is the story of a man who, as Dante's hero did, "came to [himself] in the midst of a dark wood."

I begin this chapter with Johnston's story because at this point our discussion, too, takes a turn. Until now we have focused on what is wrong with the American evangelical church. By using such terms as *the triumph of sentimentality, the new provincialism, the Christian-industrial complex, body-count evangelism,* and *the great stereopticon,* I have attempted to rightly name the diseases besetting us. And as we learn from the story of the Gerasene demoniac, the man of the tombs whom Jesus delivered from demons, by naming the disease we can have power over it.[1]

But merely naming the disease is not enough. For healing to take place, we must now prescribe a cure. Because the obvious answers are not always the right answers, let's follow the trajectory of Johnston's life a bit further.

From Parachurch to Planting Churches

If you looked at Johnston as he stood at the edge of the City Soleil slum in 1987, and you came armed with common stereotypes, you might have predicted a life of liberal social activism for him. And, indeed, many of the people with whom Johnston worked in that period of his life ended up pursuing just such a path.

So it may not seem obvious that twenty years later, Johnston—after attending seminary and becoming a priest in the Episcopal Church and a bishop in the traditionalist Anglican Mission in the Americas (AMiA)—now considers church planting to be an essential gospel work. It is an insight that took many years to germinate in Johnston's thinking, but it is an insight that a growing number of people are coming to, in part because of the failures of the religious right (on the one hand, with its megachurches and parachurches) and the religious left (on the other, with its government handouts and social programs) to effectively care for the least and the lost.

Haiti, where Johnston began his ministry career, is a case in point. No country in the world has been the object of more attention from the American church. Evangelical megachurches have sent literally thousands of mission teams. Mainline and secular organizations such as those Johnston worked for have built homes and dug wells. But today, Haiti is arguably in worse shape than it has been at any time during the past thirty years. Not only have our efforts not helped, they seem to be harming the country in significant ways.

Haiti is a particularly interesting place to observe because the country shares space on the island of Hispaniola with the Dominican Republic. With similar culture, geography, climate, and natural resources, we might expect the countries to be remarkably similar in both Christian influence and economic development; but that is not the case. The Dominican Republic is by no means prosperous, but it has a per capita gross domestic product four times that of Haiti. Virtually every cultural indicator in the Dominican Republic, including the number of Christian believers, is higher there. Such statistics have caused J. L. Williams, the founder of the Christian ministry New Directions International and an expert on Christian work in Haiti, to wonder if "what we are doing is not part of the solution, but part of the problem."[2]

Find 'Em, Fool 'Em, Forget 'Em: The Rise of Short-Term Missions

Everything we have so far discussed about the megachurch and the parachurch could be used to support J. L. Williams's melancholy conclusion. The desire for the quick fix, the disregard for history and culture, and the forgotten ability to discern with any spiritual depth are all symptoms of the new provincialism and the triumph of sentimentality. And they have become precisely not only the way the modern megachurch and the parachurch practice religion but also the way they now do missions, which is not primarily with a long-term commitment to people, but with the so-called short-term mission trip.

Robert Priest has studied the growth in short-term mission projects. He is a professor of mission and intercultural studies at Trinity Evangelical Divinity School. Priest said that "the number of lay people in the United States involved in short-term missions grew from an estimated 540 in 1965 to 22,000 in 1979. By 1989 it had grown to an estimated 120,000. Three years later the figure had doubled to 250,000. It is now estimated that there were at least one million short-termers in 2003."[3] A significant reason for the explosive growth in short-term mission trips is the growth of the Christian-industrial complex, which now includes travel agents who specialize in such mission trips, promoting them in the same way that group tours are promoted, by giving discounts to participants and free accommodations to the local organizers, often pastors or youth directors.

But just because there are many people going doesn't mean that there is a lot being done on these trips. Indeed, Priest said that "the shift to short-term missions is significant, [in that] it may be the first mission movement in church history that is based largely on the needs of the missionary."

In fact, Bob Lupton believes it is possible that these short-term mission trips have a detrimental effect. Lupton has spent a career ministering to the poor, mostly in inner-city Atlanta. His book *Theirs Is the Kingdom*, about a life of ministry to the poor, has become a minor classic. Lupton believes that microlending and church and community-building programs run by indigenous people are more effective than short-term mission projects. He wrote about one such program, run by Opportunity International, that "offers small loans to peasants in underdeveloped countries to assist them in growing their grass-roots businesses."[4] It has been highly effective in getting people on their feet in Nicaragua. Brittany Smith, in an October 19, 2006, op-ed for the Evangelical Press News Service, takes up the story:

> Because of these positive changes Lupton asked his tour guide, Juan, who is also the director of Opportunity International, "Where does the church fit into all of this?" Juan at first tried to dodge the question but finally he admitted that Nicaraguan churches that had church partnerships with the United States were "destroying the initiative of the people." He went on to explain that "entrepreneurship declines as dollars and free resources flood in [from these churches]. [People] become conditioned to wait for the next mission group to arrive

instead of doing the hard work of building their businesses." He told how dignity is eroded as people come to view themselves as charity cases for wealthy visitors.

Lupton went on to describe the way the pastors of these foreign churches had become tour guides. Lupton said, "Nicaragua has disturbed me. It calls into question the way the Western church does mission. Surely we know better than to spoil a culture with our kindness. We know that doing for others what they can do for themselves is fundamentally hurtful—to both giver and recipient. We must find a better way."

Smith concluded that among the better ways of doing short-term mission projects is to work at home and send the money saved by not traveling overseas. Indeed, indigenous pastors in India, Haiti, and many African countries support their families on less than one thousand dollars per year—less money than the cost of airfare to go visit them.

So, to return to the question with which we started this chapter, Is anyone doing it right? Johnston, as I said, came to believe that church planting is at the heart of gospel work. He turned down offers of pastorates at large churches to plant a biblically orthodox Anglican church in Little Rock, Arkansas. When that church grew to self-sufficiency, with several hundred members, he moved to Charleston, South Carolina, to begin the process again. He's left not only his law career behind but also opportunities for megachurch power. "I could be happy planting churches the rest of my life," he said.

So is this "getting it right"? Johnston would be the first to tell you that he makes mistakes every day. Indeed, all organizations are made up of people, so no one is doing it perfectly; but the church-planting work Johnston is now engaged in is a vocation being followed more and more by people who have tried the Christian-industrial complex—and found it wanting.

That's why I want to spend most of the rest of this chapter examining the work of an organization that has been intentional about working outside of the Christian-industrial complex. As a consequence, it went virtually unnoticed for the first twenty years of its existence; but it is now becoming a large church-planting movement that cannot be easily dismissed by those wanting to know what works and what doesn't work.

That organization is Gospel for Asia.

Not Just Addition, Multiplication

In many ways, Dallas-based Gospel for Asia (GFA) began out of the same megachurch and parachurch phenomena that we have spent much of our time together examining. But GFA's founder, K. P. Yohannan, saw the pathologies of the Christian-industrial complex and has continued to graciously and firmly refuse to participate in them.

Yohannan's own story is an inspiring one. I heard much of it directly from him when I visited him in 2006 in the South Indian state of Kerala, not far from the village in which he was born.

Yohannan made a profession of faith at age eight, and committed himself to full-time Christian ministry at the age of sixteen. Yohannan's early ministry work was with Operation Mobilization, a large and sometimes controversial ministry that had just begun operating in India. But the young Yohannan knew he needed more theological training, and he eventually found his way to the United States, to Dallas and Criswell Bible College, where he was its first international graduate. Yohannan had already resolved, however, that he wanted to go back to his native India. So he started Gospel for Asia in 1979 with his wife, Gisela, when they were both still in their twenties, to provide the structure to support native missionaries in India and later all of southern Asia.

Yohannan had seen one of the nation's best-known mega-churches at close range when he was at Criswell Bible College. Indeed, W. A. Criswell, the school's founder, might be called the pastor of the postwar evangelical movement. Criswell became senior pastor at Dallas's First Baptist Church in 1944 and remained in that role until 1995, more than fifty years. During that time, the church grew to more than twenty-five thousand members. Criswell was twice president of the Southern Baptist Convention and is considered the patriarch of the conservative resurgence in the Southern Baptist Convention and of the growth in political clout of the religious right. In 1976 Criswell actively campaigned for Republican Gerald Ford over Democrat Jimmy Carter, even though Carter was a Southern Baptist and Texas had been until then solidly Democratic.

If W. A. Criswell was GFA's spiritual father, Operation Mobilization might be said to be GFA's spiritual mother. Yohannan was just a teen when he fell under the influence of George Verwer, who is often credited—or blamed—with the growth in short-term mission projects.

Verwer was born again at a Madison Square Garden crusade of Billy Graham in 1955, and that experience had a profound impact on his life. He immediately started distributing gospel tracts at his high school and soon after went on an adventure to Mexico with some of his buddies. He said that trip opened his eyes to the fact "that God could use even young people in a foreign country."[5] Verwer and his friends began making trips all around the world, including one to the Soviet Union in the summer of 1961. Verwer was arrested and accused of being a spy. He was ultimately released, but the experience became the catalyst for the creation of Operation Mobilization, which was based in London but quickly grew and sent young people all around the world. Operation Mobilization's work expanded to India, and a teenage K. P. Yohannan became a part of it.

But if K. P. Yohannan saw the genius of these men and their ministries, he also saw their limitations—or at least the limitations of the approaches they took. And from the beginning, Yohannan resolved to build neither a megachurch nor a megaministry.

At its core, Gospel for Asia is a ministry that supports native missionaries who plant indigenous churches. While Gospel for Asia works with a wide variety of indigenous churches, its closest association is with the Believers Church of India. The Believers Church has divided the region into dioceses, each with its own leader. So whether this language sounds episcopal or presbyterian in polity, it is thoroughly conservative and evangelical in doctrine.[6]

When a new church is planted by the Believers Church, it operates under the oversight and with the authority of the diocese. Since the overwhelming majority of Believers churches start literally from scratch, often in villages where there are no Christian believers, it is impossible to have true elders, since all new converts are necessarily new Christians and do not immediately fulfill the biblical requirements for eldership. However, as the church grows and the new converts mature, elders are named. Over time, some of the new church's members will attend Bible college. Eventually, enough new churches will be planted in a region, each one producing Bible school prospects, to warrant the building of a new Bible college in the region. In this way, the cycle starts slowly, perhaps with only one or a few church plants in a region, but before too many years, a few church plants produce a Bible college that in turn produces many church plants. The net result is a multiplication of churches, a multiplication of new believers, and a multiplication of Bible colleges.

But it's not a multiplication of power and infrastructure. In fact, Believers Church, as of the end of 2006, had planted about thirty thousand churches with 1.7 million Christian believers as members. There were over sixty three-year Bible colleges in the country, with thousands of new church planters—most of them first-generation Christians—graduating each year. All this in the past thirty-five or so years. The Believers Church is almost certainly the fastest-growing Christian denomination in the world today. It's possible that it is the fastest-growing Christian denomination in history.

In chapter five, when we discussed body-count evangelism, we quoted megachurch pastor Rick Warren at some length, explaining how his Saddleback Church had grown to 23,500. However, it is also hard not to compare the Rick Warren megachurch model to the K. P. Yohannan multiplication model. Warren's Saddleback Church and Yohannan's Gospel for Asia were founded within months of each other in the late '70s. As we revealed, Warren's estimate of 23,500 members is almost certainly inflated, and there is some evidence that the church is now actually in decline. The Believers Church, by using its "small is beautiful" church-planting strategy, sees its growth rate accelerate with each passing year. For even though the average size of a Believers church is less than one hundred people, the sheer pace of the church planting and the rate of conversions mean that the Believers Church of India is growing at the rate of about ten Saddleback churches per year.

The strategy of GFA/Believers Church means that they receive no missionaries from the United States or any other country—not even short-term missionaries. In fact, though the budget of Believers Church of India/GFA is now more than $50 million per year, that comes out to less than $2,000 per church. Indeed, the Believers Church has less than two hundred staff members who are involved in anything resembling administration, and that includes the administration of the Bible colleges, the Believers Church seminary in Tiravalla (one of the largest in India), and the growing Bridge of Hope children's program, which now works with over fifty thousand children on a daily basis.

The Power of Love

K. P. Yohannan is not a man looking to build an empire, but there is a strategy, an orderliness, and a clear hierarchy to the ministry's work that is worth examining in greater detail.

Because the Believers Church/GFA leaders are mostly young and homegrown, this clarity gives them an opportunity to succeed in their leadership roles. The Bible colleges all over the country, for example, teach the same curriculum. The courses begin with basic Christian doctrines and include spiritual warfare and hermeneutics—principles of Bible interpretation. Though the biblical languages of Greek and Hebrew are not taught, English is. Indeed, though the churches operate in indigenous languages, English is the lingua franca of the Believers Church. Because many Christian converts come from the lowest castes and because English is the language of government, commerce, and therefore the upper castes, teaching English to the students is transformative in their lives.

Simon John leads the Northwest India diocese, which includes Delhi and seven other states with a population of 350 million people. I met with him, though, in the high-tech city of Hyderabad, a city of more than a million closely packed people in the central part of the country. Simon John is, in some ways, the quintessential Believers Church leader. He is tall and handsome, with a full head of dark hair just lightly salted by gray. In appearance and executive presence, John would fit in comfortably in a corporate boardroom anywhere in the world. Indeed, he has a degree in finance and commerce; and his father, a successful businessman, for a time moved his family to the

United Arab Emirates, one of the most affluent and cosmopolitan countries in the world.

But what distinguishes John—and many of the Believers Church senior leaders—is his powerful personal testimony of salvation and calling to the ministry. "Though I was raised in a Christian home, I did not give my life to Jesus until I was twenty," he said. The defining moment in his conversion experience came when he visited a church where the text of the sermon was John 21:15: "Simon son of John, do you truly love me more than these?"

"Because my name was Simon and I was the son of a man named John," Simon John said with a chuckle, "I used to be afraid of that verse. So I vowed not to go back to that church the next Sunday. I went to a different church the next week, and they preached on that verse there, too. Now I am very afraid. I traveled to a church one hundred kilometers away, and they preached that verse in that church too!"

This modern-day "Simon son of John" believed that this had to be more than a coincidence. "I surrendered my life," he said. "That was a real encounter with God. I told him I would do anything, that he could send me anywhere. So God sent me to Bihar."

Bihar is a state in the northern part of India. The northern part of the country is much more hostile to the Christian faith than the southern part, for a variety of historical and political reasons. India has had an indigenous Christian church since the first century. The apostle Thomas went to India to preach the gospel, probably around AD 50, and he is buried in Chennai (formerly known as Madras), in the southern part of the country, a few hundred miles south and east of where I interviewed Simon John. Many centuries later, the Portuguese established significant settlements in southern India, bringing with them Catholicism. A few towns in southern India still have communities that speak Portuguese.

But the influence of Christianity has not been widely felt in the northern part of the country, and Bihar came to be known as the "graveyard of missionaries" because of the difficulty the church had in establishing a foothold there. But this is where Simon John believed God was sending him. So in 1994, at the age of thirty, taking a wife but leaving a promising career, he went.

He settled in Bihar, and his days then were filled with simply walking the streets, passing out gospel tracts, and talking with people. "I would pray, 'Lord, fill me with the lostness of people.' I would not eat until I had shared with thirty to forty people in a day. Sometimes it would be 4 or 5 PM before I would have my first meal." He said he was not really fasting, in a conventional sense. "I just could not enjoy food until I had shared with as many people as I could," John said.

When people would decide to follow Christ, he would often send them to a Believers Church; so within a year John came under the GFA umbrella of support and accountability. Today, he leads the diocese that includes Bihar. It also includes twelve hundred churches, thirteen Bible colleges, and sixty-seven Bridges of Hope programs.

Eschewing Emotionalism

After meeting with Simon John in Hyderabad, we drove a few miles outside of the city to see Gospel for Asia's largest Bible college. This school sat on thirty-three acres and had 388 students in residence on the campus and another 200 being served remotely.

The leader of the Hyderabad facility and my guide for the day was B. Moses. Like Yohannan, Moses began his ministry career with Operation Mobilization, serving there for seven years. Like Simon John, he paid his dues as a church planter in remote villages. "We slept along the roadside," he said. "Sometimes in cemeteries. We would go without food."

That was the essence of the Believers Church. They did not conduct large evangelistic rallies. They eschewed emotionalism. As I spoke with B. Moses, he stood up from his chair, which was behind a simple wooden desk. On the desk was a telephone, but no computer. Moses had previously told me that this office, on the second floor of an open-air brick building, got so hot in the summer that he could not work from there during many months of the year. But, fortunately for me, I was visiting with him in October, and the weather had started to cool. He walked over to a map of India hanging on the wall, touched the map almost as if he were blessing the country, and what he said next could just as easily have come from the mouth of Jonathan Edwards: "My joy is to see people hear the gospel. A clear presentation. To accept the gospel is the work of the Holy Spirit. He will do his business when we do our business."

After spending much of the day at the Bible college, we drove yet farther out of Hyderabad. We were fully into the countryside in that part of India where most of the thirty thousand Believers Church churches have been planted. The road turned to dirt in places. Ox-drawn carts were a primary mode of transportation, and they often clogged the road in front of us. So it took thirty minutes to cover the short six-mile distance, but we eventually came to a small village. We stopped in front of the Believers Church, a small but sturdy building with a cross prominently reaching skyward from the peak of the church. The pastor of the church—whose name we promised not to use for reasons that will become apparent in a moment—came out to greet us and invite us in. We sat in plastic chairs as he told us, with the help of a translator, yet one more remarkable story in a day filled with remarkable stories.

When he first came to this village to plant a church, he often slept out in the open at the end of long days spent going from house to house, distributing literature provided by the Believers Church. He met much resistance and once was beaten severely by radical Hindus in the town. During that beating he had teeth knocked out, and his ear was nearly ripped off. But the pastor persisted. And when the village began to experience a water shortage, they drilled a well next to the road in front of where the church would eventually be.

"Everyone told us the well would not bring water," he said. "But we prayed, and by God's grace and for his glory the water came." The pastor let it be known that it was Jesus who had brought the water, and he called the well the Jesus Well. He also let it be known that everyone in the village, even those who had beaten him or who had been happy when he was beaten, could freely use the well.

"Seeing the water from the well changed the hearts of many people," the pastor said. Soon a few were coming to the Believers Church for services, and before long thirty and then forty and then fifty people were coming. The pastor explained to these new church-goers that their attendance at church would not save them. Only by turning from their sins and accepting Jesus would they be saved. Eventually, ten people made that decision, but because it was soon after the pastor had been beaten, he—and others in the leadership of the Believers Church, including B. Moses—decided that it would be safer if they were baptized at the Bible college in Hyderabad.

The first ten who were baptized were followed by more who made the decision to follow Jesus. B. Moses said that now, every Sunday, sixty-five people crowd into this small Believers Church for worship.

A View of Eternity

But do these stories about T. J. Johnston, K. P. Yohannan, and others actually prove anything?

We have applied—I hope—clearheaded logic to the mega-church and the Christian-industrial complex, so we should, in fairness, do no less here. And in so doing we must point out that church planting is a risky activity. A ministry can claim to have planted thirty thousand churches. A skeptic might ask how many survived to self-sufficiency and self-replication. These are fair questions. And certainly these anecdotes are not intended to be unalloyed praise of either Gospel for Asia or the Anglican Mission in the Americas. Because these organizations are made up of fallible human beings, they are not perfect; and no doubt a close examination, or even a not-so-close examination, would reveal flaws.[7]

Neither are they meant to be a case for complete abandonment of all evangelistic and discipleship enterprises except church planting. God's tapestry is made up of many threads. To use biblical language, there are many members of the body of Christ, and they are each vital to its health.

So the experiences recounted here are not meant to be representative, but suggestive. That said, though, I think you can see—especially given the context we have spent seven chapters building—they are not merely suggestive but richly suggestive of a possible future that the evangelical church needs to pay more attention to.

Those possibilities came into sharp focus just a few days after I returned from my tour of India. In God's providence, soon after I arrived home I received a copy of *Outreach* magazine's annual list of the one hundred largest churches in the United States. The entire issue was devoted to these churches and their pastors. I couldn't help but notice that the largest church was feel-good preacher Joel Osteen's Lakewood Church. I also noticed that recently disgraced Ted Haggard's New Life Church was number thirty-seven on the list.

This issue was the one I used for many of the statistics I quoted in chapter five. But more to the point for our discussion here, this issue brought into clear focus the contrast between the mega-church approach and the smaller, humbler, yet ultimately more consequential approaches I have attempted to describe here.

As I read through that issue, I also couldn't help but think about the churches I had seen and the pastors I had met in India—pastors who had given up everything and had in some cases[8] been beaten nearly to death—and about T. J. Johnston, whose background and top-drawer education, including a law degree, could have allowed him to live a life of affluence, social status, and ease.

But it would be a mistake to call these men saints or even selfless. They were building something, and there was something in it for them, too. But that something they were building was something that might not show up for a generation. It was work done with a view not to what can be seen in the present, but what would result over time and what would last into eternity.

So as I compared what I had seen in India to the model of church growth touted in the issue of *Outreach* magazine and by so many others in evangelicalism, a stark contrast made itself manifest, a contrast that motivated this question: Which model is more authentic, more biblical, more likely to produce fruit over time?

I am, of course, being a bit coy even to ask the question. For after seeing Ted Haggard in tears on television and comparing that image to my memory of those pastors in the remote villages in India, shedding tears of a different kind, it's a question I no longer ask of myself.

My mind is made up.

CHAPTER 8

TRUE RELIGION

The missionary work of the non-professional missionary is to live his daily life in Christ, and therefore with a difference, and to be able to state the reason and cause of the difference to men who see it. His preaching is essentially private conversation, and has at the back of it a life which explains and illustrates and enforces his words. It is such missionary work that the world needs today. Everybody, Christian and pagan alike, respects such work. When it is so done, men wonder, and inquire into the secret of a life which they instinctively admire and covet for themselves.

—ROLAND ALLEN (1869–1947) IN *NON-PROFESSIONAL MISSIONARIES*

Large areas of "the World" will not hear us till we have publicly disowned much of our past. Why should they? We have shouted the name of Christ and enacted the service of Moloch.

—C. S. LEWIS IN *THE FOUR LOVES*

There is no such thing as a post-Christian society. One generation may reject the Gospel itself, but it cannot reject it for future generations.

—LUIS PALAU

So what have we learned? And given what we have learned, how should we then live?

There is a great temptation—and a great danger—in reducing the answer to that question to a memorable but vacuous rubric. That is precisely what the Christian-industrial complex has done with every aspect of the Christian life, and we get an endless supply of disposable "McBooks"—books like John Maxwell's *21 Irrefutable Laws of Leadership*. Why not twenty? Why not twenty-two? And, more to the point, why wasn't Jesus smart enough to make things this easy to remember?

The answer to that question is what Jesus knew and wanted us to know: following him isn't a formula or a checklist. Mnemonic devices and lists have their places. Many biology students remember "King Phillip, come out, for goodness' sake" as a way to remember the classification system: kingdom, phylum, class, order, family, genus, and species. But too often, we Christians create the mnemonic first and then look for the system that fits it.

That's why I'm reluctant to reduce the journey we have been on to a single set of principles that would solve the problems of modern evangelicalism. When Michael Card was asked for a solution to the problems facing the Christian music industry, especially its loss of community and its tendency to turn art into a profit center, he wisely refused to offer a single, succinct prescription. "That's part of the problem," he said. "We want it to be one thing. Because we want to be able to do that one thing and then be off the hook or declare it done. To check it off the list. But it's not just one thing."[1]

Rodney Stark came to that same conclusion in *The Rise of*
Christianity. Sociologist Stark relied on history and logic to piece
together events and disparate data sets to construct a fascinating
portrait of the growth of Christianity in the first few centuries of
the church. Here is the problem Stark confronted: "Finally, all
questions concerning the rise of Christianity are one: How was
it done? How did a tiny and obscure messianic movement from
the edge of the Roman Empire dislodge classical paganism and
become the dominant faith of Western civilization? Although
this is the only question, it requires many answers—no one
thing led to the triumph of Christianity."[2]

It's not just one thing. So while I do not want to create a
checklist, I do think it is worth looking at some of the ideas
we've explored in this book to see if somewhere there is a path
back from the deep woods we have entered.

The Rise of Christianity

There are few better places to start on this path back than
Stark's book. It does much violence to his fascinating study to
reduce it to a single idea; but it is fair to say that the book is
Stark's attempt to explain one of the mysteries of the growth of
the church, and that is the explosive growth of Christianity in
the third century.

Most evangelicals, if they think about the rise of the early
church at all, imagine that its growth was the result of evangelistic efforts, particularly the mission trips of the apostles.[3] The
problem with this theory is that it fails to account for how the
church actually grew in the first four hundred years after the

birth of Jesus. The very few numbers we have in the Book of Acts indicate a church that is growing. Acts 1:15, describing a time just a few months after the resurrection of Jesus, gives us a very specific number of Christian believers: "In those days Peter stood up among the believers (a group numbering about a hundred and twenty)." The resurrection must certainly have created a stir in Jerusalem, but it apparently did not create an immediate harvest of converts.

However, the preaching of the gospel and the selfless living of the church described in Acts 2 and elsewhere were having an impact on Jerusalem. By Acts 4:4 we learn that "many who heard the message believed, and the number of men grew to about five thousand." Even so, Stark used a variety of biblical and historical sources to conclude that the number of Christians in the known world was only about 7,500 by the end of the first century. By the end of the second century, the number of Christians had risen to about 200,000. This is a great increase in absolute numbers, but it still represented a very small percentage of what was likely a population of sixty million in the Roman Empire of that time. Stark also pointed out that it represents a 3.42 percent growth rate per year. By way of context, Stark said that the Mormon church has maintained a growth rate considerably faster than that over the past century.[4]

But even by the year AD 250, with Christians now numbering more than a million, they still represented less than 2 percent of the Roman Empire's total population and were the subject of widespread persecution. Even by the mid-third century, church buildings were virtually nonexistent. The Christian church was largely a home-church movement. Persecution made large-scale rallies impossible. But something remarkable was happening. Even as the church passed the one million mark, even without significant communication among churches in neighboring cities, the historical growth rates continued. An inexorable 40 percent per decade growth rate turned one million Christians in AD 250 to six million Christians by AD 300. By the year AD 350, Christians made up a majority of the Roman Empire—an estimated thirty-four million people.

How did this fantastical growth occur? Again, it was not by using the tools that the modern evangelical church places so much stock in—media, communications, and mass rallies. The growth of the early church came about by less glamorous means. Because Christians cared for one another, they lived longer and were therefore able to better care for their own children. Their children were more likely to survive childhood diseases and reach childbearing years. Also, in a culture where infanticide—especially of girls—was common, Christians took in girl babies from non-Christian families. As a consequence, Stark estimated that the Christian community may have been 60 percent female in the second and third centuries.[5] The number of females in the surrounding pagan cultures was lower by a commensurate percentage. In other words, the shortage of eligible females in the pagan cultures motivated many men to convert to Christianity in order to marry Christian women.

A second and related reason for the explosive growth of Christianity was the loving care given by Christians to their brothers and sisters in the Lord. Late in the second century, around AD 165, a great epidemic hit the Roman Empire, a catastrophe sometimes called the Plague of Galen. It's possible that 25 percent of the Roman Empire perished in this plague. Another great plague struck the empire about a hundred years later. Death became a clear and present danger for Christians and non-Christians alike. But the response of Christians and pagans to these plagues could not have been more different. Dionysius, an Egyptian bishop of the Coptic Church from AD 248 to 264, wrote a moving letter that has become famous among historians but is little known by modern evangelicals. This letter beautifully testifies to the posture of Christians of the era and says much to explain why many Christians survived the plagues and why many non-Christians looked at the church with awe and wonder.

> Most of our brother Christians showed unbounded love and loyalty, never sparing themselves and thinking only of one another. Heedless of danger, they took charge of the sick . . . ministering to them in Christ, and with them departed this life serenely happy; for they were infected by others with the disease, drawing on themselves the sickness of their neighbors and cheerfully accepting their pains. Many, in nursing and curing others, transferred their death to themselves and died in their stead. The best of our brothers lost their lives in this manner, a number of presbyters, deacons, and laymen.[6]

Rodney Stark's well-documented analysis of the growth of the early church involved much more than just these factors, but it does not overstate the case to say that the majority of the growth of the church in the first four centuries could be attributed to the fact that Christians had larger and healthier families than adherents of other religions. And when the children of Christians reached adulthood—because they had been raised in the nurture and admonition of the Lord—they firmly embraced the faith of their fathers.

The Growth of the Old Order Mennonites

It's easy to dismiss Stark's account of the rise of Christianity in the first few centuries as an interesting history lesson without much applicability today. However, such a glib dismissal would be to ignore some modern analogues.

I have already mentioned the Mormons, because in the twentieth century they embodied the same growth trends that the early church demonstrated and for much the same reason: they had large families that successfully transmitted their faith to the next generation. And there is another, even more interesting analogue embodied in the Old Order Mennonites.

Old Order Mennonites are also known as "horse-and-buggy" or "Wenger" Mennonites, named after former Bishop Joseph Wenger. The group gives us a unique opportunity to look at a rapidly growing religious group in the modern era that has almost completely eschewed modern church-growth techniques. In fact, the group owes its creation to this disdain for modernity. The Old Order Mennonites got their start when about two hundred families, in 1927, split from other Mennonites who wanted to allow the use of automobiles.

According to sociology professor Donald Kraybill, there are now eighteen thousand Wenger Mennonites in nine states, with most living in rural areas such as the Finger Lakes region of New York and parts of Lancaster County, Pennsylvania. Kraybill said there are two reasons for the growth. First is the high fertility rate of the Old Order Mennonites. They have more than eight children per family. Second is the intensive discipleship of children. Nearly 90 percent of their young people stay in the religion when they reach adulthood. These factors have resulted in the group doubling in size every eighteen years since it was formed.[7]

Kraybill reported some new pressures on the group. For example, the group has grown so fast that it owns most of the land in its home region. Extended families are buying land farther and farther from the original homesteads, a phenomenon that makes it tough for these families—who won't drive automobiles—to maintain family cohesion. Nonetheless, Kraybill estimated the fundamentals of high fertility rates and strong spiritual formation practices will keep the growth rate strong for years to come.

So does this entire discussion amount to little more than recovering obedience to God's command to be fruitful and multiply? In some ways, the answer to that question is a resounding yes. But what does fruitfulness for the evangelical church look like? That is the question we will answer in the rest of this chapter, the answer that brings our discussion to a close.

Church Planting: Bigger Is Not Better

The early church Rodney Stark described and the rapidly multiplying church we read about in the last chapter—the

Believers Church of India—were both essentially church-planting organizations. Indeed, church planting seems to be an essential core competency for any religious body that wants to be fruitful and multiply.

It's a core competency that some modern churches have discovered. Take the Presbyterian Church in America (PCA) as a conspicuous example. The PCA was formed in the late 1970s when many Presbyterians could no longer tolerate the liberal drift of the mainline Presbyterian Church (USA).

It is a small denomination in absolute numbers, with only about 300,000 members in 2003. But it has wielded enormous influence in the evangelical world for the past thirty years for two reasons. The first reason is its rate of growth. Though the size of the denomination is small, in the last thirty years, no Protestant denomination in the United States has received more members or planted more churches than the PCA. Second, the denomination has some of the most high-profile pastors and churches in the country. D. James Kennedy and his Coral Ridge Presbyterian Church, which had a major radio and television presence until Kennedy's death in 2007, were a part of the PCA. Joel Belz and Marvin Olasky of WORLD Magazine, the nation's leading evangelical newsweekly, are both PCA elders. In 2003 Belz was the moderator of the denomination's General Assembly, its annual national convention. The conservative, Calvinist theology of the PCA is rapidly—some would say—becoming the theology of modern evangelicalism.[8]

Redeemer Presbyterian Church, in Winston-Salem, North Carolina, is part of this denomination and has been enjoying that growth, too. But the pastor and elders of that church made an important decision. They would not grow above five hundred members, a milestone they were rapidly approaching. "Bigger is not better," said its founding pastor, Rev. Clyde Godwin.[9] "In big churches, people become spectators, and Sunday morning services become a show. We want to be a church of disciples who worship and serve. For what we're trying to create, smaller is better." Their goal? As they approach five hundred members, they will ask if some in the congregation will plant new churches, far enough away to be in a different community and serve people the mother church can't serve, but close enough so that the mother church can continue to provide financial and other support, as needed.

Godwin claims that church plants have three times more adult conversions than other churches. Since making that decision, his church has been instrumental in planting a half-dozen churches in the region. Godwin continues his church-planting efforts for the PCA.

The Presbyterian Church in America, the Anglican Mission in the Americas, and Gospel for Asia/Believers Church are not, of course, alone in their church planting zeal. I cite these three groups because church planting is not merely a strategy, but is central to their organizational identity. It's not what they do, but what they are.

Why? I think it is because they have rediscovered the following important truths:

It Produces More Opportunities for Ministry

Megachurches often tout their ability to offer more ministries. But it is ministry using the industrial model, taking advantage of economies of scale, rather than ministry using the community model, taking advantage of people's gifts and calling. In a large church or large parachurch organization, the level of skill required to manage the organization must necessarily be high. People with less leadership ability, or developing ability, often are reduced to spectators. That's one reason why a Christian can sit in the pew of a megachurch for years and be able to offer no more leadership to his family, community, or church than when he first walked through the church's door.

It Produces Greater Accountability

The modernist worldview rejects the doctrine of original sin. Modernist and progressivist worldviews that have been dominant since the Enlightenment teach the notion that people are basically good, that we can be anything we want to be, that we should reach for the stars, and that the sky is the limit. By now, we should recognize this as the heresy of Genesis 3: "You will be like God." We should recognize it, but we do not. And, despite protestations to the contrary, some modern megachurch and parachurch organizations are also based on this worldview.

Human organizations, especially Christian organizations, should have strong systems of accountability built in. The larger the organization, the harder these systems are to implement and maintain. The responsible exercise of power requires great character. The leader of a large organization simply has more power than most people have the character to control. And in large organizations, those around the position of power have too much to lose if they confront the senior leader and the senior leader does not respond appropriately to that confrontation. So these confrontations rarely take place until they become scandalous.

The Ted Haggard scandal is by no means the only example, but it is in some ways emblematic. Here is a man who led not only one of the largest megachurches in the United States but also the National Association of Evangelicals. He essentially had no one he was accountable to. Because his nondenominational church operated outside the bounds of any ecclesial authority, he was free to do what he wanted—and he did, being called to account only when his private behavior became known to the world.

It's Multiplicative

One of the most interesting aspects of a healthy living system is that its growth tends to be multiplicative, not additive. Scripture clearly commands us to be multiplicative, not additive. "Be fruitful and multiply," as we have observed, is one of God's first commands to humans.

The megachurch is an example of an additive system. It adds people to its own membership, but it rarely multiplies itself. That's one reason we can see the number of megachurches growing, while the overall number of churches and the total number of Christians either remain flat or are in decline. In fact, it is unfortunate that perhaps the most apt metaphor for the megachurch's relationship to the body of Christ is that of the cancerous tumor: as it grows, it kills the body.

A multiplicative system, on the other hand, starts out slowly and—because multiplication is in its DNA—accelerates in growth over time. Gospel for Asia, for example, seemed to grow slowly in its first decade, but that was because it was following a model in obedience to the command to be fruitful and multiply. Just as individuals must reach puberty to have the biological maturity for fruitfulness, so organizations must bring their members to a spiritual puberty before they can be spiritually fruitful. That takes time and the right kind of nutrition. But when it happens, the growth is multiplied. This year, for example, Gospel for Asia will plant more churches than it did in the first ten years of its ministry. Stark's account of the early Christian church showed a similar pattern.

Habitat for Humanity is an organization that has multiplication built into its DNA. When it builds a house for someone, it requires the new homeowner to pay back the money spent on the house and to invest "sweat equity" in the building of both their house and others' houses. Both money and labor are multiplied. The result is that Habitat will build more houses this year than it did in the entire first decade of its existence.

Megachurches and large parachurches, on the other hand, tend to have growth curves that are exactly the inverse of those organizations based on multiplicative models. They grow rapidly in the beginning and then level off or even decline. As we saw in chapter five, for example, Rick Warren's Saddleback Church saw a decline in membership in 2005. Now, not all declines in membership are bad. Flat or negative growth can be a good thing if people are intentionally sent out to plant other churches, as in the case of Clyde Godwin's church in Greensboro. Another church in the PCA denomination, Perimeter Church in Atlanta, has grown significantly under the leadership of pastor Randy Pope, and it has also intentionally planted more than a dozen autonomous PCA churches in the Atlanta area.

It Demonstrates a Dying to Self

For a growing church to intentionally plant another church, which inevitably has the effect of reducing its own size and financial resources—at least temporarily—is an act of sacrifice and humility. For the leadership of a church to make such a decision sends a powerful message to the congregation that its goal is not the accumulation of power or wealth, but the enlarging of the kingdom of God. When Friendly Hills made the decision to plant a new church when it reached five hundred members, it was also making a decision that it would not have some of the things that only large churches can have. For the leadership of such a church, that translates into giving up income and, often, political and denominational influence. But it is hard to imagine, if God's Word about such matters is true, that such an intentional dying to self will not yield fruit. In 1 Corinthians 15:36 Paul explained that a seed will not germinate unless it first dies. The multiplying of the church appears to require a similar death; but it is a particular kind of death, the death of personal ambition, a relinquishing of what Friedrich Nietzsche called the "will to power."[10]

It's Biblical

Jesus clearly had the ability to draw large crowds, but almost invariably he retreated from them, in favor of the more intimate relationships he had with his disciples. A story that makes this point, and several others we have been discussing, is the story of the Gerasene demoniac, or the man of the tombs, told in three of the four Gospels. We have already mentioned this story, but it's worth a closer look.

At about the midpoint of Jesus' ministry, after preaching to large crowds on the northern shore of the Sea of Galilee, Jesus wanted to leave the crowds behind. Mark 4:35 takes up the story: "That day when evening came, he said to his disciples, 'Let us go over to the other side.' Leaving the crowd behind, they took him along, just as he was, in the boat."

Jesus went to a region on the southeastern shore of the Sea of Galilee, and there he encountered a man who lived among the tombs, possessed by demons. Jesus asked the demon its name, and the demon replied, "My name is Legion, for we are many." And then something interesting happened. After the demon told Jesus his name, "he begged Jesus again and again not to send them out of the area." Somehow, by knowing the demon's name, Jesus had power over it. Said more accurately, the demon's yielding of his name seemed to be an act of submission to Jesus' power.

Jesus cast the demons out of the man and into a herd of pigs, which ran into the sea and drowned. The demoniac regained his right mind and wanted to follow Jesus, but Jesus again did something most remarkable as Julie Miller noted in chapter four: he told the man to stay behind. Jesus knew that the one place on the planet where the demoniac's transformation wouldn't need to be explained was right where he was. The people who knew him before would know that something miraculous had happened.

So what are the lessons from this story for us? First of all, we see that Jesus left the many to minister to the one. Second, we again see the power in the right naming of things. Third, we learn in Jesus' instructions to the man to stay behind the power of the transformed life. Jesus knows—and wants us to know—that it is not status and power that attract the world to the gospel, but the truly transformed life.

The Recovery of Vocation

In the 1990s a business book about corporate decision making and change made the rounds. It was called *Five Frogs on a Log* and was based on a simple riddle: "Five frogs were sitting on a log. One decided to jump off. How many frogs were left?" The natural temptation is to answer four. But the authors make their point with this answer: "Five. Because deciding to jump and actually jumping are two different things."[11]

The problem with the evangelical church today is that the kind of transformation evident in the life of the Gerasene demoniac is not evident in the lives of most Christians today. And the kind of sacrifice that Dionysius wrote about during the plagues of the third century is also not much in evidence. In other words, one of the reasons our evangelistic efforts fail today is that we are not thoroughly evangelized ourselves. We may have made a *decision* to follow Jesus, but we are not—most of us—*really following* him.

That is not to say that God does not use flawed vessels. He does. And I want to be careful not to advocate a kind of

Heretical! too bold! o

modern-day pharisaism as a biblical replacement to the lively but sometimes heretical theology of the modern evangelical church.

What I am advocating, in a nutshell, is an understanding that in God's economy, theology is biography. Knowing God is sovereign and acting as if God is sovereign must be the same thing for the true Christian disciple. Jesus said this when he said that to love God is to love our neighbor (Matthew 22:36–40) and to receive forgiveness we must forgive (Matthew 6:9–13).

In the end, I am trying to make this point evident: discerning and following God's calling on our lives is both the primary mission of the individual Christian as well as the most significant step we can take toward bringing healing to the body of Christ. Said another way, God knits together the body in his wisdom and sovereignty. That which is most healthy for the individual members is necessarily that which is most needful for the body.

It should therefore be equally evident that one of the surest signs that the evangelical church has succumbed to the spirits of the age—which we defined in chapters two through six—is the state of disrepair into which have fallen our conversations regarding vocation.

As I suggested above, instead of teaching our children to discover their gifts and discern their calling, we instill the notion that they can grow up to be anything they want to be. Since at least the days of Lincoln, it has been common to tell small children that "in America, anyone can grow up to be president." When we also reflect on the fact that most of us consider the president of the United States to be the most powerful person in the world, we begin to understand that, however unintentionally, we are succumbing to the same false promise offered to Adam and Eve by the Serpent—that we can be like God.

We do this with all good intentions, of course. But, as I said at the beginning of chapter six, whether we succumb to this heresy intentionally or are merely lured into it as into a trap by the entertainment culture, the results differ little. And when it comes to our vocational life, we end up not doing our work heartily, as to the Lord, but doing our work grudgingly and planning for an early retirement. (See Colossians 3:23–24.)

Indeed, the modern ideas of retirement and the midlife crisis are symptoms of this loss of vocation. Because others[12] have written wisely about the economic, spiritual, sociological, and cultural issues surrounding these modern phenomena, I will not attempt to explicate them here, except to observe that if we are pursuing work that brings sustenance and fulfillment, we would not question its value. We seek to retire from or have a crisis about those things that debilitate us, not those things that maintain and elevate us.

At the core of our loss of vocation is the sense that work itself is somehow demeaning, rather than ennobling. We forget, for example, that the Bible explicitly calls God's creative acts "work": "By the seventh day God had finished the work he had been doing" (Genesis 2:2). In other words, we are following God, imitating God, most closely when we are involved in creative work.

This idea should be foundational to a Christian worldview. Yet Christians are as lost as non-Christians when it comes to matters of vocation; indeed, perhaps more so. We have turned work into a necessary evil. And Christians too often get sucked into prosperity-gospel theology and secular get-rich schemes that have been overlaid with a thin veneer of Christianity. Multilevel marketing schemes, in particular, promise the possibility of building a business that ultimately produces income without work, as if that were a good thing even if it were possible.

Working for money alone or as a means to an end (for retirement, for leisure, or even for time to "do ministry"), rather than working as an act of worship, produces all kinds of perverse results. For one thing, on a purely practical and economic level, the pursuit of money by some of us makes the pursuit of vocation by any of us more costly and therefore more difficult. For starving artists to eat, they must buy bread at the price millionaire investment bankers are willing to pay for it. In other words, people who pursue wealth "bid up" the cost of living for us all.

The result is that most people feel they are forced to work for the love of money and not for the glory of God or to exercise their God-given talents and calling. This melancholy reality is surely the great destroyer of vocation today.

The Recovery of Community

So how is vocation discerned and nurtured? The short answer is this: in community with other believers likewise attempting to discern and nurture their vocation. A. J. Conyers in his book *The Listening Heart: Vocation and the Crisis of Modern Culture* helps us see this relationship between vocation and community.

The familiar term *vocation*, used in religious and secular contexts, is rooted in the Latin *vocation*, meaning "call," and is related to Latin-based words such as *voice* and *invoke*. The Greek word is *klesis* and is found in our words *cleric* and *ecclesiastical*. It is the root of the New Testament word for the church, *ekklesia*, a point that is not etymologically significant except in that assemblies of all kinds were referred to with the same term. To say that the church consists of those "called out," however, is significant for more reasons than can be traced through linguistic usage: it has been the reality to which the church has always attested.[13]

Said in language more familiar to evangelicals and others: Christians are those who are called, and the church is the body of Christ that has been called out of the world. In other words, discovering our vocation and discovering our place in the body of Christ are essentially the same pilgrimage.

We have already observed that one of the core problems we face is that often the church doesn't want to be the church. The industrial model that the modern evangelical megachurch has become has sought wealth and power. We have done this probably with the best of intentions, telling ourselves that the larger, richer, and more powerful we become, the greater impact for the kingdom we will have.

The only problem with that theory is that it is now demonstrably not true. It has been said that the problem with Christianity is not that it has been tried and found wanting, but that it has not been really tried. Whether that cliché is true or not could be a subject of lively discussion. However, it is irrefutable, given both the data and the stories we have seen here, that the industrial model of doing church has been tried by some of the smartest people in Christendom and that, while some megachurches have temporarily thrived, the church itself is in disarray. We have already recounted the data: fewer people go to church today than when the modern parachurch movement began in the aftermath of World War II. People who call themselves Christians often do not understand or believe core Christian doctrines. And those who do too often outsource the spiritual nurture of their children to youth groups and conferences. Our children are entertained and kept (temporarily) safe, but they are not challenged. They are utterly unprepared either to discern God's calling on their lives or to assume roles as leaders of their homes, their communities, or their churches. The result is that the children of the modern evangelical church often require reevangelizing as adults—and the Christian-industrial complex is, ironically, perpetuated.

It is time for a different approach. It is time for the modern American Evangelical church truly to be the body of the Incarnate Christ.

EPILOGUE

There will be visions and revisions.
—T. S. ELIOT IN *THE LOVE SONG OF J. ALFRED PRUFROCK*

You and me we know too much.
—MARK HEARD

Midway this life, I came to myself in the midst of a dark wood.
—DANTE IN *THE DIVINE COMEDY*

This kind can come out only by prayer.
Surely I am with you always, to the very end of the age.
—JESUS IN MARK 9:29 AND MATTHEW 28:20

And so we come to an end of things. But if you have persisted with me this far, you know that it is not an end of things at all. To put the matter a bit glibly, we have caught more fish than will fit in our pan.

But such is the hard reality of the intellectual and spiritual task before us in these latter days, in what Marion Montgomery has called, with some ruefulness, the "lag end of the romantic age." What he means by that, at least in part, is that we now know that our sentimental vision of the world is no longer adequate. It has played out. It is out of gas. But life nonetheless goes on, and all of the ancient rights and responsibilities remain. We really are children of God. We really are called to take dominion over the land. And we now know that the tools we need for the task—the spiritual and intellectual inheritance bequeathed to us by our fathers—we have all but squandered.

That's the bad news.

But the good news is that we did, finally, come to ourselves. Or, at the very least, we are now confronted with that choice. We are deeper in the woods than we at first thought, perhaps. But we can come to ourselves. We can awaken. And we can remember what we have been taught. In God's providence, it is never too late to do the right thing.

And most of all we remember this: God's Word and God's sovereignty over all the universe are greater and stronger than our ability to make a mess of things. He has promised that the gates of hell would not prevail against his church (Matthew 16:18). Nor would he let his word return without accomplishing what he sent it out to do (Isaiah 55:11).

That is why we can return with hope, not despair, to the image with which we started our journey together, the image of Dante in a dark wood, profoundly lost. We return to that image knowing that when he came to himself and found his way out, the story he wrote we now call *The Divine Comedy*—not *The Infernal Tragedy*.

The evangelical church may yet have to pass through the refiner's fire. My lover's quarrel with the evangelical church leaves me melancholy regarding our chances of avoiding that trial. But, as Dante teaches us, the journey through the inferno is the first part of the story, not the last.

We can take comfort in that, at least.

Introduction

1. "Ousted Evangelist Confesses to Followers," Associated Press, November 5, 2006.

2. It's interesting to browse MinistryWatch.com's website and see how many of today's major Christian ministries were founded in the 1940s and '50s. A few examples: World Vision (1950), Campus Crusade for Christ (1951), Compassion International (1952), Young Life (1941), and InterVarsity Christian Fellowship (1941).

3. It would be difficult to overstate the impact that Richard Weaver's *Ideas Have Consequences* has had on the creation of this book. In fact, my original vision for this book was to translate *Ideas Have Consequences* into "Christianese." The book that follows is both much more and much less than that, but it seems fitting to acknowledge the debt early and often.

Chapter 1: The Evangelical Myth

1. The Hartford Institute, which is associated with Hartford Seminary, does a regular study of megachurches in the United States. These numbers came from an interview the author did with Scott Thumma, the lead researcher for the 2006 study. The Hartford Institute for Religion Research at Hartford Seminary maintains an excellent website of the research, including a searchable database of megachurches. The Web address is http://hirr.hartsem.edu/megachurch/ megachurches. html. That said, researcher Thumma ultimately succumbed to the megachurch version of the Stockholm syndrome, wherein the captive begins to empathize with the captor. The book Thumma and coauthor Dave Travis wrote based on this research, *Beyond Megachurch Myths: What We Can Learn from America's Largest Churches* (The Leadership Network, 2007), is essentially a paean to megachurches, ignoring some of the more ominous implications of its own data.

2. Source: The Internal Revenue Service, cited by the National Center for Charitable Statistics, a division of the Urban Institute.

3. Source: CBA (formerly Christian Booksellers Association).

4. James Davison Hunter, *American Evangelicalism*. Identifying who is and is not an evangelical is a bit of a black art. Often, for example, different contemporary studies have different definitions of *evangelical*, and the word itself has changed meaning over time. Hunter's work traces the rise of evangelicalism from the early part of the twentieth century through the 1980s. His work is brilliant and definitive for the period he explores, and no look at evangelicalism should ignore it. But some of the data are twenty or more years old. Also, in part because of Hunter's work, more interest in the demographics of evangelicals has resulted in other data sources. In any case, for our purposes here, the data from the two different sources are consistent, if not identical.

5. *Baptist Church Planting*, April 6, 1999.

6. Ibid.

7. From a press release from the Barna Research Group dated December 1, 2003. Barna's research is almost unfailingly interesting to those of us who follow religion in North America, but it, too, is at best suggestive. For example, in this survey Barna identified a series of questions that, if answered in the affirmative, meant a respondent had a biblical worldview. To be sure, these questions related to core Christian dogma, such as a belief in a literal resurrection and the virgin birth. But identifying these questions and these questions only as indications of a biblical worldview is obviously subjective. A different set of questions, or even minor wordsmithing of the questions Barna posed, would have likely yielded very different results. Nonetheless, Barna's data are often the best we have when it comes to such matters.

8. *CPA Journal*, the *Independent Sector*, and various professional and academic papers all report a figure in the neighborhood of 7 percent. These numbers are estimates, culled from the approximately 1.6 million tax-exempt organizations that file tax returns each year.

9. In a spirit of full disclosure, I should add that my own newspaper, the *Charlotte World*, was actively involved in promoting this event. In fact, it was this event that in many ways was a turning point for me. It's not that I think that holding the rally or the ideas promoted at the rally were wrong. But in the two years that have followed, I have just come to believe that they had no impact. Or, said more precisely, the impact did not justify the time, money, and talent expended.

10. Both Michele Goldberg's *Kingdom Coming* and Randall Balmer's *Thy Kingdom Come* mentioned the rallies as significant events in the development of the "values voter" phenomenon. They also referred to the rallies in private interviews with the author. Both Goldberg and Balmer were critical of the events. (Randall Balmer, *Thy Kingdom Come: An Evangelical's Lament*, NY: Basic Books, 2006; Michele Goldberg, *Kingdom Coming: The Rise of Christian Nationalism*, NY: W. W. Norton,

2006.)

11. "Right Turn on Campus," *Atlanta Weekly*, February 20, 1985.

12. Dan Gilgoff, *The Jesus Machine: How James Dobson, Focus on the Family, and Evangelical America Are Winning the Culture War* (NY: St. Martin's Press, 2007). This book, though a bit clinical in places, is one of the best blow-by-blow accounts of the rise of Focus on the Family in particular and of what I describe in general in chapter 4 as the Christian-industrial complex.

13. In speeches and interviews, Reed tells the story of "praying to receive Jesus," sitting at a restaurant called Bullfeathers, which is two blocks south of the Capitol and just across the street from the Republican National Committee's Capitol Hill headquarters. Then and now it's a place where members of Congress and staffers can be found eating and drinking at almost any time of the day or night. It was a regular meeting place of Reed, Abramoff, and Grover Norquist during the days described here.

14. *TIME* magazine, May 15, 1995. In some ways, this was the "coming out" of Ralph Reed as the leader of the religious right. From 1982 to 1989, Jerry Falwell and the Moral Majority were the acknowledged leaders of the religious right. The Christian Coalition was formed in the aftermath of the Moral Majority's demise and with the funds left over from Pat Robertson's presidential campaign. Reed was hired to lead the group, but Robertson remained the public face of the group until it became clear to many that it was Reed, with uncommon organizational skills, communication skills, and a relentless work ethic, who really built the organization into the powerhouse it became. Both the Republican takeover of Congress in 1994 and George W. Bush's election in 2000 owe a great deal to the activism of Reed and the Christian Coalition.

15. A little-credited but key element of that campaign was a tough article about McCain in WORLD Magazine, written by Bob Jones IV. Though WORLD Magazine had a circulation of only about 100,000 at the time it did its scathing article on McCain, there were a disproportionate number of those subscribers in South Carolina. (WORLD is published in Asheville, North Carolina, just an hour up I 26 from Greenville, South Carolina, the home of Bob Jones University.) Many of WORLD's subscribers are pastors, deacons, and elders of prominent churches. The WORLD article was given an unintended boost by *New York Times* columnist William Safire, who wrote a scathing denunciation of it.

16. The attribution of this line to Adlai Stevenson may be an urban myth, since I have not been able to find a definitive attribution. The 1964 movie *The Best Man*, starring Henry Fonda and Cliff Robertson, comes very close to lifting this line verbatim. Henry Fonda played a character modeled (many say) after Adlai Stevenson. That movie, which caused

a sensation in its day, is still one of the best political satires ever put to film—though it has a decidedly liberal bias.

17. As this book was being written, Sen. Charles Grassley was investigating Hinn, Meyer, and four other televangelists. The investigation appears ultimately headed for some sort of a showdown, since some of the televangelists—Kenneth Copeland and Creflo Dollar, in particular— maintain that they are constitutionally protected from investigation by the U.S. Senate. The position of MinistryWatch.com, the ECFA, and other watchdog groups says that these organizations should be completely transparent, with or without a Senate investigation. Full disclosure: the author served as a spokesman for MinistryWatch.com during the period of the Grassley investigation.

18. Most revenue figures cited in this section came from the website of MinistryWatch.com. Ironically, Graham's compensation has come under a bit more scrutiny in recent years because of his semiretired status.

19. It is important to note that "dealt with" means fully disclosed. It does not mean these expenses were eliminated. Franklin Graham continues to draw salaries from both ministries, salaries that when combined exceed $500,000 a year. Samaritan's Purse is a tax-exempt humanitarian organization. Its supporters expect the money contributed to go directly to humanitarian aid, yet the organization earned more than $100 million (income minus expenses) in the four-year period from 2002 to 2005.

This episode, by the way, also exposed problems with the Evangelical Council for Financial Accountability (ECFA), the self-policing organization founded in the midst of the televangelist scandals of the 1970s and '80s. The formation of the ECFA likely staved off increased government regulation of parachurch ministries, but the group has proved to be an anemic watchdog. For one thing, it derives its income from member organizations, and the larger the organization, the greater the dues. So it is unlikely that a large and powerful member organization will receive any serious discipline or oversight by the ECFA. Second, only about 2,000 of the 750,000 religious nonprofits in the country are members. The "bad guys" just don't bother to join, since there is no stigma for nonmembership.

20. William Bennett is fond of saying that "the plural of anecdote is not data." That's certainly true, but sometimes the telling anecdote represents the truth more than a boatload of data, as we will see in chapter 5, "Body-Count Evangelism."

Chapter 2: The New Provincialism

1. Flannery O'Connor, *The Habit of Being* (NY: Farrar, Straus & Giroux, 1979), 444.
2. H. L. Mencken published his famous essay "The Sahara of the Bozarts"

in 1919 to decry the lack of literary and intellectual output from the states of the Old Confederacy. However, he later came to respect the robust and excellent literary production of many of the southern Agrarians and others whose output came to be known as the Southern Literary Renaissance.

3. Allen Tate, "The New Provincialism," collected in *Essays of Four Decades* (Wilmington, DE: ISI Books, 1999).

4. This letter, well known to Edwards scholars, was dated December 12, 1743. It can be found in *The Collected Works of Jonathan Edwards* and on any number of websites, including http://www.nhinet.org/ccs/docs/awaken.htm.

5. Interview with the author, September 2000. David Barton, among others, has argued that the United States could not, indeed, even exist without the spiritual and intellectual underpinnings of the Great Awakening. I would not argue that point as vigorously as Barton has in such books as *America's Godly Heritage*, but I will say that there is some evidence that this was so. I would also argue that, whether true or not, many early Americans believed that it was so and that this belief contributed greatly to their willingness to endure the privations of the early years of this nation—and has contributed greatly to the notion of American "exceptionalism" that has been a significant part of the American national psyche.

6. S. E. Morison, *The Oxford History of the American People*, Vol. 1 (Oxford University Press, 1975), 225–226.

7. We'll make a more direct connection between revivalism and cults in chapter 5, "Body-Count Evangelism."

8. There are hundreds of references in the mainstream and gay media to Oberlin's "gay friendly" reputation. One example: Blake Rehberg, "Oberlin Battles Stereotypes of Male Athletes in Sports," the *Oberlin Review*, February 23, 2001.

9. The Southern Baptist Church has no official position, though on the denomination's website you find this: "If you surveyed Southern Baptists, you would likely find many who hold to the 'Pre-Tribulational' view of the rapture, others who hold to a 'Mid-Trib' view, some to a 'Post-Trib' rapture, some who hold to historical premillennialism, and perhaps even a few who don't agree with any of these views" (http://www.sbc.net/aboutus). My own view, having been raised in a large Southern Baptist church and having covered the church as a journalist for more than twenty years, is that most Southern Baptists who have an opinion on the matter believe in a premillennial, pretribulation rapture of the church.

10. The Vatican issued the statement on July 21, 1944, in response to some

who were beginning to teach that Adolph Hitler was the Antichrist and that a millennial reign was beginning.

11. Reported by columnist Cary McMullen, NYT Regional News Group, June 17, 1999. Originally published in the *Paltka Daily News*.

12. The pastor of a Presbyterian Church in America (PCA) congregation in Charlotte, North Carolina, told me that his nearly twenty-year-old church had grown to nearly six hundred people, but during that twenty-year period the church had performed no more than a handful of funerals. "I could count them on one hand," he said.

13. Interview with the author, October 26, 2004.

Chapter 3: The Triumph of Sentimentality

1. Richard Weaver, *Ideas Have Consequences* (University of Chicago Press, 1948), 18–34.

2. Interview with the author, March 2001.

3. Forest Hill Church and Warehouse 242 have since left the EPC denomination.

4. The phrase *regular attender* is one of the terms of art of the megachurch and church-growth movement. The number of regular attenders is the number most often reported when a megachurch is asked questions about its size. At least two megachurches I reported on while the publisher of the *Charlotte World* achieved that status (more than two thousand regular attenders per weekend), while admitting to a true and active membership—which required a profession of faith—of less than three hundred people. (These churches are Mecklenburg Community Church and Elevation Church.) More on this phenomenon in the chapters ahead.

5. The *Charlotte Observer*, December 11, 2001, page 1-B. After Hahn's breakdown, he left the ministry for several years to become a corporate trainer, consultant, and speaker. He quietly reentered the ministry as a pastor of a nondenominational church in Charlotte, North Carolina, called Next Level.

6. West Barrington is one of the most affluent communities in the nation. According to the U.S. Census Bureau, the median household income was in excess of $170,000 per year. (The national median household income was less than one-third of that number.) As of the 2000 census, the town of South Barrington, Illinois, was about 82 percent white, and most of the rest (about 14 percent) were Asian.

7. *Outreach* magazine publishes an annual list of the largest churches in the country. These numbers were taken from that list, published in the July/August 2005 issue. However, these lists are compiled from numbers that are reported by the churches themselves, and, as we will see in chapter 5, this process is badly flawed and by its nature encourages churches to

overreport.

8. The attendance and membership figures of Mars Hill Bible Church have been called into question by critics of the emergent church movement. Mars Hill was planted by another megachurch in the Grand Rapids area, Calvary Church. Calvary's long-time pastor Ed Dobson retired in 2005, and at least some of the growth at Mars Hill can be attributed to membership declines at Calvary.

9. G. A. Pritchard, *Willow Creek Seeker Services: Evaluating a New Way of Doing Church* (Grand Rapids: Baker Books, 1996).

10. Don Cousins, *Tomorrow's Church . . . Today* (South Barrington, IL: Willow Creek Publications, 1979). Cited in Pritchard, 32.

11. Pritchard, *Willow Creek*, 32.

12. Ibid., 33.

13. Mike Breaux often describes his work this way. One example: his presentation to the Student Ministries Conference, March 2, 2004.

14. This quote from Jim Rayburn is so widely quoted both inside and outside of Young Life that I can't find an original reference, though it is likely that he first said it in the 1940s.

15. Pritchard, *Willow Creek*, 89.

16. Ibid., 287.

17. Randall Balmer's book *Thy Kingdom Come: An Evangelical's Lament* suggests that the rise of Christian colleges was driven at least in part by racism. He particularly noted Bob Jones University's conflicts with the Internal Revenue Service in the 1970s over the school's ban on interracial dating. However, this conclusion doesn't fit the data. Most Christian colleges in the United States were founded in the nineteenth and early twentieth centuries. It's true that some famous Christian colleges (Liberty University, Bob Jones University, Oral Roberts University, and Regent University) came specifically out of the evangelical movement, but race does not seem to have been the driving factor. Oral Roberts University, in particular, is much more diverse than most state universities.

It's true that Bob Jones had policies that forbade interracial dating, and those policies attracted national attention. But the real issue seems, to most fair-minded observers, to be more about the ability of the school's administration to control policies than about race, per se. Interracial dating was merely the particular policy over which the battle was fought.

In any event, the case that ultimately decided the issue of government funding and control had nothing to do either with Bob Jones University or with race. The Grove City College case—fought over the college's refusal to sign government nondiscrimination policies based not on race but on religious grounds—ultimately went all the way to the

U.S. Supreme Court in the late 1970s. Grove City College lost the case and decided to completely separate itself from all government funding and all requirements to comply with government regulations associated with that funding. In the years that followed, the college thrived. In an interview with the author, Dr. Richard Jewell, the president of Grove City College, said, "We may have lost the battle, but we won the war. There are now more than 2,200 laws and regulations that pertain to colleges and universities that accept government funding." Jewell said that complying with these regulations is a "manufactured cost" and is one of the reasons for the steep escalation in the cost of higher education. Grove City College, on the other hand, has a tuition about half that of other academically comparable colleges.

18. Lauren Winner recounted the story in a November 13, 2000, posting on the *Christianity Today* website.

Every year, a few dozen folks from Willow Creek Community Church make a pilgrimage to 121 Kellogg Place in Wheaton, Illinois—the home of Gilbert Bilezikian and his wife, Maria. The pilgrims pass a sunporch where Bilezikian, the theologian behind Willow Creek, spends most of his time in the summer and fall.

"We built that porch a few years ago, right where Bill Hybels drove his motorcycle the day he came to see me in 1975," Bilezikian says of his former student, who would become the church's senior pastor. The Willow Creek pilgrims make their way to the backyard, past Maria's elaborate flower garden and the tomato and cucumber plants her husband tends ("I am better known for my salads than for any theological work I've ever done," he notes, only half in jest), to the spot where Willow Creek was born.

"Right here," says Bilezikian, standing in the middle of his lawn. There Hybels, then no more famous than any other recent college grad, roared up on his bike and said, "Dr. B., you and I are going to start a church."

19. Jamie Dean did much of the reporting on the section that follows. Jamie was the editor of the *Charlotte World*, which I published, during a season when we did a number of articles on Osteen and the megachurch phenomenon.

20. To put this number in context, the average church in the United States has less than three hundred members. Though it must also be said that in most megachurches, no more than half who attend the services of the churches are actually members of the churches. However, neither are they—as megachurch proponents claim—unchurched. More often than not, "regular attenders" are actually members of other nearby churches. Indeed, one of the criticisms of Lakewood and other megachurches is that they "suck all the air out of the room." In other words, they

turn men and women who could fulfill leadership roles in smaller churches into spectators in their more difficult-to-penetrate leadership teams. (Though in the case of Willow Creek, Lakewood, Rick Warren's Saddleback Church, Robert Schuller's Crystal Cathedral, and other megachurches led by celebrity pastors, as many as 30 percent are actually out-of-town visitors, "spiritual tourists," making one-time trips to the church.)

21. All comments from Liichow are from an interview with Jamie Dean, used here with permission.

22. All quotes from Michael Horton in the section that follows are the result of personal interviews either with the author or with Jamie Dean. All quotes not the result of interviews with the author are used with permission.

23. *Larry King Live*, June 20, 2005. Transcript available at www.cnn.com. The second interview was with Joel Osteen and his wife, and it aired October 16, 2007.

24. The comments on Joel Osteen were posted by Mohler on his Web log on September 8, 2006. They can be found at www.almohler.com.

25. Joel Osteen, *Your Best Life Now* (NY: FaithWords, 2004). Cited by Jamie Dean, "Positively Dangerous," the *Charlotte World*, February 4, 2005.

26. Ibid.

27. Cited by Jamie Dean, "Positively Dangerous," the *Charlotte World*, February 4, 2005.

28. FaithfulReader.com. Cited by Jamie Dean, "Positively Dangerous," the *Charlotte World*, February 4, 2005.

29. Richard W. Weaver, *Ideas Have Consequences* (University of Chicago Press, 1948), 21. (This page number from the 1976 Midway edition.)

Chapter 4: The Christian-Industrial Complex

1. In a spirit of full disclosure, I should say that I did not originate this expression. I first heard my friend Steve Beard, the driving force behind the website www.thunderstruck.com, use this phrase. Though a Web search turns up hundreds of hits on the phrase, some of them predating both Steve and me.

2. Posted on Joel Rosenberg's blog, December 1, 2004: www.joelrosenberg.blogspot.com.

3. Statistics are all over the board in this area, depending on who does the measuring and what is being measured, but these numbers are consistent with those offered annually by CBA and the Gospel Music Association.

4. Interview with the author, October 26, 2004.

5. Cited in "Deliver Us from Branson," by Warren Smith, Evangelical Press News Service, June 21, 2006.

6. Interview with the author, June 2007.

7. Interestingly, Mark Ward Sr., in the official history of Christian broadcasting commissioned by the National Religious Broadcasters for the fiftieth anniversary of that organization, leaves out this interesting factoid. (*Air of Salvation: The Story of Christian Broadcasting*, Grand Rapids: Baker Books, 1994.) However, it is well documented elsewhere. Canadian inventor Reginald Fessenden broadcast from Brant Rock, Massachusetts, a recording of "O Holy Night" and read a passage from Luke 2. The broadcast, which had been publicized by shortwave radio, was listened to by ships up and down the Atlantic Coast.

8. Parts of the section that follows were originally published by the *Charlotte World* and the Evangelical Press News Service as "Targeting Becky." All quotes from Joe Paulo are the result of interviews with the author. ("Targeting Becky," by Warren Cole Smith, the *Charlotte World*, August 5, 2005.)

9. *TIME* magazine, February 2, 2005. It is interesting to note that of the twenty-five people on the list, only two are what you might call theologians—Richard John Neuhaus, a Catholic, and J. I. Packer, an Anglican. One of them, Dianne Knippers, has since died; and another, Ted Haggard, has since been stripped of his position as a result of a sex and drug scandal. You could make a case that these facts reflect more on *TIME* magazine's judgment than on the state of evangelicalism, but I think that ignores the reality that leadership in American evangelicalism has become a cult of celebrities. We no longer follow the suffering servant, but the successful one.

10. The third-century Origen said that it was unseemly to celebrate the birth of Jesus as though he were a "king pharaoh." Indeed, the celebration of all birthdays was more or less condemned by Christians as a prideful veneration of the self. (For more information on the history of the Christmas celebration, see also "The Real Story of Christmas" at www.history.com/minisites/christmas/.)

11. William Bradford, the first governor of Massachusetts, required men to work on Christmas Day. When new arrivals said that they would not work as a matter of conscience, Bradford excused them from the requirement "until they were better informed." (Records of the General Court, Massachusetts Bay Colony, May 11, 1659.)

12. Religion News Service, December 21, 2006.

13. Much of this section is the result of several conversations and interviews with Michael Card between 2002 and 2007. Some of these interviews are archived at www.thecharlotteworld.com. In a somewhat unrelated but nonetheless interesting note, Card's "El Shaddai" was named one of the 250 most influential songs of the twentieth century by the Recording Industry Association of America.

14. It is important to note, though, that discipleship and artistry are not the same thing. Not all great artists are good people. But it is fair to say that all good people live their lives with a certain artistry.

15. Mallonee also worked with Mark Heard, a man who perhaps more than any other held in his body and in his music the tension between art and money, industry and community that we've been talking about in this chapter. Alas, that tension—the sheer emotional, spiritual, and financial difficulty of trying to reconcile these two worlds—might have been a contributing factor in his death. He had a heart attack while performing onstage at the Cornerstone Festival in 1992 and died a few weeks later, at age forty. It is perhaps worth noting here, discussing as we are artists who have not renounced Christianity but who can't find a comfortable home in the Christian music ghetto, that the price Mark Heard, Bill Mallonee, Julie Miller, Michael Card, and others have paid—often financial costs that make family and other relationships more stressful—means that there are a few broken-down wrecks by the side of this road. I don't know if that is inevitable, but it is understandable. Like Jacob, if you wrestle with an angel, you're likely to get a blessing, but you're also likely to get your leg broken. For the true Christian artist, it's one of the costs of discipleship, a cost made greater by knowing the cost in advance. The title of one of Mark Heard's own songs—"You and Me We Know Too Much"—captures the dilemma most well.

16. Milton's *Areopagitica*. Legend has it that John Milton was the last man alive who "knew everything." In other words, through reading and study and life experience he knew everything that mankind's knowledge had up until then accumulated. His assessment that his audience was and would remain "fit, though few" was in part an assessment of the gap between those who study deeply the "causes of things" (*causus rerum*) and those who do not.

Chapter 5: Body-Count Evangelism

1. Mark Cahill, *One Thing You Can't Do in Heaven* (Rockwall, TX: Biblical Discipleship Ministries, 2002).

2. All of these figures are from MinistryWatch.com, which posts the financial statements of the five hundred largest Christian ministries in the country on its website.

3. I say "only" merely as a comparative term, not as a term of judgment. In fact, an important theme of this book is that, as E. F. Schumacher wrote, "Small is beautiful." A congregation with ninety adults and a more or less requisite number of children to go with them has a much better chance of developing a culture of accountability and leadership than does the spectator culture of the megachurch.

4. Robert Bellah et al., *Habits of the Heart: Individualism and Commitment*

in American Life (Berkeley, CA: University of California, 1985), 167.

5. The surge in religious piety in the Boston region had at least one interesting consequence that is also in some ways emblematic of the point I am making: it forced the young Benjamin Franklin, a deist and freethinker, to quit the town and move to Quaker-dominated Philadelphia. Indeed, H. W. Brands's biography of Franklin (*The First American: The Life and Times of Benjamin Franklin,* NY: Random House, 2000) appropriately begins not with Franklin's birth, but with the culture into which he was born—the Massachusetts colony under the pervasive influence of the Puritan Cotton Mather.

6. Marvin Olasky, *The Tragedy of American Compassion* (Washington, DC: Regnery, 1992).

7. The total number of tax-exempt organizations in America in 1998 was almost 1.4 million, *CPA Journal*, June 2002. The number continues to grow. *CPA Journal*, the *Independent Sector*, and various professional and academic papers all report a figure for employment in the neighborhood of 7 percent. These numbers are estimates, culled from the approximately 1.6 million tax-exempt organizations that file tax returns each year.

8. The Leadership Network is a group that promotes church growth and leadership development of church leaders. The group sometimes cites the number 300,000 churches in the United States and 350,000 churches in North America, presumably including Canada.

9. See chapter 2, note 5.

10. The professional theologians in the crowd are probably howling at this statement. The truth is that the theologically learned on both sides acknowledge that, in general, the great struggle going on for the theological center of evangelicalism is this struggle between Calvinism and Arminianism. Few modern Christian theologians, however, claim to be Arminians, for precisely the reason mentioned: the Arminian notion of free will leads inevitably to heresy. The argument, therefore, generally becomes one of "how Calvinistic" one is. A recent debate at the Southern Baptist Convention, for example, featured Dr. Al Mohler, a "five-point Calvinist," and Dr. Paige Patterson, a "three-and-a-half point" Calvinist.

11. The "utter depravity" of humanity is one of Calvin's five points. Here they all are, expressed in the form of the acronym for which they have become famous among theologians: TULIP. Total depravity, Unconditional election, Limited atonement, Irresistible grace, and Perseverance of the saints.

12. Karl Menninger, *Whatever Became of Sin?* (NY: Hawthorne, 1973). Menninger wrote, "The very word, 'sin,' which seems to have disappeared, was once a proud word. It was once a strong word, an

ominous and serious word. But the word went away. It has almost
disappeared—the word, along with the notion. Why? Doesn't anyone
sin anymore? Doesn't anyone believe in sin?" http://docjohns.blogspot.
com/2007/11/whatever-happened-to-sin_13.html.

13. The Second Great Awakening is well documented in a number of
excellent books. The basic facts as I outline them for the next few
paragraphs are not much in dispute, though their meaning continues to
be hotly debated. For an academic and sociological look at this period in
our religious history, see Roger Finke and Rodney Stark's *The Churching
of America, 1776–2005*, second edition (New Brunswick: Rutgers
University Press, 2005). For a biography of Charles Finney, the defining
figure of the Second Great Awakening, that is for my money a bit too
sympathetic but commendably thorough, see *Charles Grandison Finney:
Revivalist and Reformer*, by Keith J. Hardman (Syracuse University Press,
1987).

14. Interview with the author, 2002.

15. Dr. Michael Horton accumulated the opinions of evangelical leaders
regarding Finney in an essay "The Disturbing Legacy of Charles Finney."
Here is the opening paragraph:

Jerry Falwell calls him "one of my heroes and a hero to many
evangelicals, including Billy Graham." I recall wandering through the
Billy Graham Center some years ago, observing the place of honor
given to Charles Finney in the evangelical tradition, reinforced by the
first class in theology I had at a Christian college, where Finney's work
was required reading. The New York revivalist was the oft-quoted and
celebrated champion of the Christian singer Keith Green and the Youth
With A Mission organization. He is particularly esteemed among the
leaders of the Christian Right and the Christian Left, by both Jerry
Falwell and Jim Wallis (*Sojourners Magazine*), and his imprint can be
seen in movements that appear to be diverse, but in reality are merely
heirs to Finney's legacy. From the Vineyard movement and the Church
Growth Movement to the political and social crusades, televangelism,
and the Promise Keepers movement, as a former Wheaton College
president rather glowingly cheered, "Finney lives on!"

16. Charles G. Finney, *Memoirs of Reverend Charles G. Finney* (NY: Fleming
H. Revell, 1876), 51.

17. Charles G. Finney, *Revival Lectures* (Grand Rapids: Fleming H. Revell,
1993), 5.

18. Finney, *Memoirs*, 368.

19. Hardman, *Finney*, 448.

20. "R. C. Sproul: Willing to Believe," an interview with Sproul by Arsenio
Orteza for *The Wittenburg Door*, Issue 161, Nov/Dec 1998.

21. Ibid.

22. Finney, *Memoirs*, 629–632.
23. B. B. Warfield, *Studies in Perfectionism*, 2 vols. (NY: Oxford, 1932), 2:26–28.
24. That would be any language that could be construed as teaching that the ordination of women was not acceptable. From the Cumberland Presbyterian Church website: http://members.aol.com/mleslie598/timeline.html.
25. The history in this section depends heavily on Roger Finke and Rodney Stark's fascinating *The Churching of America, 1776–2005*, second edition (New Brunswick: Rutgers University Press, 2005). See especially chapter 3, "The Upstart Sects Win America, 1776–1850," and chapter 5, "Methodists Transformed, Baptists Triumphant."
26. Ingrid Schlueter, "Billy Graham Will Not Say If a Good Jew, Muslim, Buddhist, Hindu or Secular Person Will Make It into Heaven," *Christian Worldview Network*, August 9, 2006.
27. "Yes to Possibility Thinking," Show number 1426, May 31, 1997.
28. I explored this tendency of megachurch leaders to fabricate or overstate attendance numbers in a December 1, 2007, article for WORLD Magazine called "Numbers Racket." The problem, as I laid it out in that article, is twofold. First, the churches tend to overreport their numbers, and, second, most journalistic outlets accept the numbers at face value. *Outreach* magazine each year publishes lists of the largest and fastest-growing churches. *Outreach* is careful to note that these are self-reported numbers, but the magazine often fails to compare this year's numbers to the numbers it published in its own pages the year before. It is common to find a church that has a *lower* attendance this year than last year but nonetheless is listed on the "Fastest Growing Churches" list.

This is exactly what happened at Saddleback during the 2004 and 2005 years in question here. The 2005 list—which covered 2004, the period about which Warren wrote—listed Saddleback's weekly attendance at 23,194. *Outreach* also said that Saddleback had grown by 2,608 during that time. That would put attendance in early 2004, at the time Warren asserted attendance at 23,500, at closer to 21,000. These are big numbers, to be sure, and we might charitably attribute them to rounding errors or imprecision, probably not rising to the level of a breach of integrity. But then the 2006 *Outreach* list was published. Saddleback listed 20,595 as the attendance number. That's a *drop* of nearly 3,000. But if you flip the page, you'll discover something even more puzzling. Even though Saddleback's weekly attendance fell by 3,000, it reported a gain of 1,149 for the year! How does a church that loses 3,000 report a gain of over 1,000? A classic example of the triumph of sentimentality: seeing the world as you would like it to be rather than as it is.

It is also worth noting that following publication of this WORLD

Magazine story, *Outreach* replaced its editor and published a revised list that corrected some, but not all, of the errors of the original list.

29. Website: http://www.theamericanchurch.org. The American Church Research Project is the brainchild of Dave Olson, who said his "research grew out of [his] frustration that no one really knew how the American Church was doing, and instead Christian leaders were often making wild guesses and declarative statements based on inaccurate hearsay. Exaggerating the challenges, overestimating the progress, or ignoring reality have been common Christian responses to the missional challenges for Christians in the United States. This research was undertaken because we cannot know where to go and how to get there until we find out where we are and why we are in that situation." His work is a fascinating, idiosyncratic, and insightful look at data that other "church growth" consultants and researchers ignore, often because they have a financial self-interest in telling a particular story.

Chapter 6: The Great Stereopticon

1. C. S. Lewis, *The Screwtape Letters* (NY: Macmillan Company, 1958), 11. Karl Marx famously wrote *The Communist Manifesto* while a young man in the library stacks of the British Museum. Some Lewis scholars have speculated that Lewis is humorously or ironically referring to Marx in this passage.

2. Neil Postman, *Amusing Ourselves to Death* (NY: Viking Penguin, 1985), Introduction.

3. Ibid., 56.

4. By making this observation I am not necessarily defending one form over another. I am simply observing that these shifts, which often end up being enormously disruptive to current power structures, are often merely the inevitable consequences—both good and bad—of new technologies.

5. Several accounts of the rise of Christian radio exist, though not one of them rises to the level of being definitive. Writing the definitive account may not be possible, given the state of flux in the industry and the uncertainty about both the impact and the ultimate state Christian radio will take. The best of several adequate but not excellent accounts is Bob Lochte's *Christian Radio: The Growth of a Mainstream Broadcasting Force* (Jefferson, NC: McFarland, 2006). This anecdote and much of the next few paragraphs are summarized from that book and Ward's *Air of Salvation*, cited earlier.

6. Ward, *Air of Salvation*, 56.

7. Sam Tanenhaus, "*Whitaker Chambers: A Biography*" (NY: Modern Library, 1997), 456.

8. Audrey Barrick, "Study: Churches Slow to Adopt New Technology,"

the *Christian Post*, April 30, 2008. I can't resist noting that this reporter missed the lead, as they say in the news business. The real story is that churches adopt new technology extraordinarily quickly, much more quickly than they understand the impact of the new technology on their theology, liturgy, and community. The moral of the story is not, however, that this reporter—a Christian reporter at that—missed the lead, but that all media, by their nature, have a bias for progress. The new thing is the newsworthy thing. Despite the fact that technological progress, the Internet in particular, is making the newspaper business challenging, the truth is that—as a general principle—change can never come fast enough for the media.

9. The Worship and Technology Initiative was a "three-year research program to study, analyze, and develop resources for the thoughtful use of presentation technology in worship." Website: www.calvin.edu.

10. Umberto Eco, *The Aesthetics of Thomas Aquinas* (Cambridge: Harvard University Press, 1988), trans. Hugh Bredin, 48. The place to go to drink your Aquinas "straight up, no ice" is, of course, his *Summa Theologica*. But that document is not for the faint of heart, and I will confess that I have never read it straight through. (Indeed, I don't think I would trust many who said they had.) My favorite Thomist is Marion Montgomery, who understands Aquinas deeply and writes about him wisely. Sometimes called by others one of the "second-generation" Fugitive-Agrarians, Montgomery calls himself a "hillbilly Thomist," as did his friend Flannery O'Connor. Regarding the matter at hand: Montgomery's *Romantic Confusions of the Good: Beauty as Truth, Truth as Beauty* (London: Rowman & Littlefield, 1997) is as good a place as any to wade into the deep waters he has explored in a sixty-year career that has (so far) produced nearly fifty books, plays, novels, and compilations.

11. Postman, *Amusing*, 56.

12. Ibid.

13. Marshall McLuhan is a fascinating and in some ways a perplexing figure. He was a deeply committed Roman Catholic after converting to the faith as an adult. His work is best understood as a critique on the modern media and celebrity-driven culture, but he cultivated—or at least did not discourage—his own celebrity. He was "adopted" as the muse or guiding force by *Wired* magazine, and there are several Web shrines to him on the Internet.

14. "The Playboy Interview," *Playboy*, March 1969. Ironies in this passage abound. For example, that pornographic *Playboy* would sit in judgment of Hitler. But that is a discussion for another day.

15. Marshall McLuhan, *Understanding Media* (London: Routledge and Kegan Paul, 1964), iv.

16. John Murphy, writing for the online publication www.catholicfiction.net. Search: "moviegoer."
17. Postman, *Amusing*, 9.
18. One story, apparently apocryphal, since I can find no reliable documentation, is that the leader of the band R.E.M., Michael Stipe, at first refused to do music videos because they resulted in what he called "intellectual fascism." In "R.E.M. Debuts New Video Clip at Concert" (by Nekesa Mumbi Moody, Associated Press, June 20, 2008), Stipe calls the music video a "dead medium," which is a remarkable pronouncement to make just twenty-five years after the medium's birth. Stipe, though, has always been of two minds about this matter, criticizing the medium while at the same time making award-winning videos. But that is its irresistible, "siren-song" appeal. Even those being drawn to it (such as Stipe) are well aware of its ability to disable other art forms and the judgment of the viewer.
19. David F. Wells, *No Place for Truth* (Grand Rapids: Eerdmans, 1993), 184.

Chapter 7: Christianity's Next Small Thing

1. In this story, Jesus asked the demon possessing the "man of the tombs" its name. The demon replied, "My name is Legion, . . . for we are many." So it is today. We will spend more time with this story, which is one of the most compelling and dramatic in all of the Gospels, in chapter 8.
2. Author interview with J. L. Williams, March 2006.
3. Cited in "Short-Term Mission Trip, or Donor-Paid Vacation?" by Brittany Smith (Evangelical Press News Service, October 19, 2006).
4. Ibid.
5. Author interview with K. P. Yohannan, October 2006.
6. Polity refers to church governance. For our purposes, I group all churches into one of three forms of church governance: episcopal, presbyterian, or congregational. Episcopal churches are governed by bishops or "episcopates," presbyterian churches are governed by elders or "presbyters," and congregational churches are self-governed.
7. As one of my mentors once said to me: "When I want to see evidence of original sin, I just look in the mirror."
8. The story I recounted above was just one of several I heard from victims of great persecution. And, of course, they are not uncommon to anyone who has studied the current worldwide missions environment. Occasionally, one of these stories of persecution or even martyrdom penetrates the news media's consciousness, as did the murder of Australian missionary Graham Staines and his two sons in Orissa, India, in 1999. But the vast majority go unreported. They are not, however,

without positive effect on the body of Christ. As Tertullian said: "The blood of martyrs is the seed of Christians."

Chapter 8: True Religion

1. Author interview with Michael Card, April 2006.
2. Rodney Stark, *The Rise of Christianity* (Princeton University Press, 1996), 3.
3. This inability or unwillingness for modern evangelicals to focus much on church history before the Reformation is, of course, one of the symptoms of the new provincialism we have already discussed. But it is also a great scandal of the modern evangelical church for another reason, and that reason is that it perpetuates the great schisms of history. In my view, one of the true signs of revival in the modern church would not be a great evangelistic rally in which many were "saved," but a great summit of church leaders from the Roman, Eastern, and Protestant worlds—a twenty-first-century Council of Nicea. At such a summit these leaders would confess and repent of attempts to discredit each other, and they would produce a creed of commonly held beliefs.
4. Stark, *Christianity*, 7. He estimated that the Mormon church maintained a growth rate of about 43 percent per decade for more than a century. And while the Mormon church is certainly known for its door-to-door evangelism, the primary engine of its growth has been the size of Mormon families. Anyone who has ever been taught the "miracle of compound interest" knows that a steady growth rate produces outsized absolute growth over time. This phenomenon is the source of the French children's riddle about lily pads. If the number of lily pads in a pond doubles each day, and one lily pad ultimately covers the entire pond in thirty days, on what day is the pond half-covered? The answer: day twenty-nine. It takes twenty-nine days to cover half the pond, but only one day to cover the other half.
5. Stark, *Christianity*, 126.
6. Cited by Stark, 82. Dionysius of Alexandria is considered one of the dominant religious figures of the third century. He was bishop of Alexandria, in Egypt, for nearly twenty years. He issued an annual Easter, or Festal (festival), letter, which was an innovation in its time. Only fragments of the originals survive, but they were quoted widely by others, notably Eusebius, the great church historian of the late third and early fourth centuries.
7. Author's interview with Dr. Donald Kraybill, Elizabethtown College, October 4, 2006.
8. A close examination of the theological rifts in the Southern Baptist Church—which are often characterized as a "liberal-conservative" or "moderate-conservative" split—are in reality arguments between those who promote Reformed/Calvinist theology and those who promote

Armininian or "Baptistic" theology. That's why some of the moderate/
liberal groups in the SBC sometimes prefer to be called "heritage"
groups. They maintain that they are the ones holding to true Baptist
teaching, and the conservatives have embraced Calvinism. Interestingly,
many of the conservatives agree. At the 2006 meeting of Southern
Baptists, a debate over this very issue arose, with Dr. R. Albert Mohler,
one of the Southern Baptist Convention's most formidable theologians
and the president of the denomination's flagship Southern Seminary,
taking the banner of the Calvinists.

9. Interview with the author, November 2000.

10. The "will to power" is considered one of Nietzsche's most important
ideas. The phrase appears in many of his books but most prominently
in *Beyond Good and Evil* (1886). Nietzsche is seen as an enemy of
Christianity, famously declaring that "God is dead." And he was certainly
no advocate of the church or of biblical Christianity. But it is also fair to
say that the demonization of Nietzsche by even some modern Christian
writers is visceral and pragmatic, and misses a larger point. Consider, for
example, the full context of his "God is dead" declaration. "God is dead.
God remains dead. And we have killed him. How shall we, murderers
of all murderers, console ourselves? That which was the holiest and
mightiest of all that the world has yet possessed has bled to death under
our knives. Who will wipe this blood off us? With what water could we
purify ourselves? What festivals of atonement, what sacred games shall
we need to invent? Is not the greatness of this deed too great for us? Must
we not ourselves become gods simply to be worthy of it?" (Nietzsche, *The
Gay Science*, Section 125.)

11. Mark Feldman et al., *Five Frogs on a Log* (NY: HarperCollins, 1999).

12. I have found Lee Hardy's *The Fabric of This World* (Grand Rapids:
Eerdmans, 1990) particularly helpful along with A. J. Conyers's *The
Listening Heart* (Dallas: Spence Publishing, 2006). Dorothy Sayers's
classic essay "Why Work?" is often anthologized, and for good reason.
Darryl Tippens's *Pilgrim Heart* (Abilene, TX: Leafwood, 2006) has
provided nourishment for me recently.

13. A. J. Conyers, *The Listening Heart*, 12. I can't resist adding a personal
testimonial for this book, which was published in 2006. Not only does
it contain some of the wisest writing about vocation and community I
have ever read, but it is also among the most beautiful and courageous
books I have read in a long while, knowing as I do that its author
succumbed to cancer at age fifty-eight, after the completion of the
manuscript but before the book itself was published. It is a book that,
among its many virtues, demolishes the new provincialism, written as it
was with a strong sense of eternity.

INDEX